Ching's
Chinese Food
in Minutes

CHING-HE HUANG

HarperCollins*Publishers*

HarperCollins*Publishers*
77–85 Fulham Palace Road
Hammersmith, London W6 8JB
www.harpercollins.co.uk

First published by HarperCollins in 2009

10 9 8 7 6 5 4 3 2 1

Photographs © Kate Whitaker 2009
Styling: Wei Tang
Food styling: Annie Nichols

Incidental images © Shutterstock pp: 5, 6, 7, 11, 12, 13, 19, 20, 26, 30, 32, 33, 35, 44, 48, 52, 54,
56, 57, 58, 62, 71, 73, 76, 82, 83, 84, 86, 89, 90, 103, 106, 118, 119, 120, 122, 126, 128 (top), 131,
136, 139, 141, 142, 144, 146, 151, 167, 181, 182, 184, 193, 194, 196, 199, 202, 205, 212, 214, 216.

A catalogue record of this book is
available from the British Library

ISBN 978-0-00-726500-8

Printed and bound in Great Britain by
Butler Tanner & Dennis, Frome

This book includes references to nuts and recipes including nuts, nut derivatives and nut oils.
Avoid if you have a known allergic reaction. Pregnant and nursing mothers, invalids, the elderly,
children and babies may be potentially vulnerable to nut allergies and should therefore avoid
nuts, nut derivatives and nut oils.

Mixed Sources
Product group from well-managed
forests and other controlled sources
www.fsc.org Cert no. SW-COC-1806
© 1996 Forest Stewardship Council

FSC is a non-profit international organisation established to promote the
responsible management of the world's forests. Products carrying the FSC
label are independently certified to assure consumers that they come
from forests that are managed to meet the social, economic and
ecological needs of present and future generations.

Find out more about HarperCollins and the environment at
www.harpercollins.co.uk/green

Introduction v
Buying & Caring for Your Wok xiii

Soups & Starters 1

Pork 23

Chicken & Duck 41

Beef & Lamb 65

Fish 79

Shellfish 95

Vegetarian & Side Dishes 115

Noodles & Rice 133

Desserts & Drinks 157

Easy Entertaining 173

Ching's Menus 206
The Store Cupboard 210
Glossary 211
Index 217
Acknowledgements 221

Introduction

When I was little I often stayed with my grandmother in Taiwan, and I have many memories of her cooking up a meal in minutes when we were hungry, and of my mother cooking several dishes with speed and teaching me in no time. I was always impressed that delicious, healthy food could be prepared and cooked easily and quickly.

These days life is so frenetic and busy that after a day's work the last thing you may want to do is slave over a hot stove. I know the feeling. There have been extremely demanding periods throughout my working life when I didn't have time to cook and it left me incredibly unhappy. So now, no matter how busy I am, I always find the time to prepare food, because it lifts my spirits, and there is no doubt that my collection of quick dishes has been my lifesaver throughout the years. Friends are always asking me for the quickest recipes or meal solutions to feed their families and so I wanted to share them with you.

I love experimenting and so, as well as including in this book all my reliable recipes that have served me well in the past, I have also created new ones. My cuisine is, of course, Chinese and I must admit that we have a head start in terms of cooking at speed. There is nothing faster than cooking a stir-fry in minutes in a wok over high heat – and nothing is more pleasurable and satisfying. However, I think 'cooking in minutes' doesn't just imply literally 'in minutes'; for me it is about the whole 'time', that is how you spend time and the process of it. Therefore, not all of the recipes may seem fast in terms of speed, but I hope you will enjoy the 'time' cooking them because they are designed to be relaxing and fulfilling.

I didn't always enjoy cooking when I was growing up in my teens. I had to cook for my father because my mum was away a lot, and she would teach me several dishes at a time before she went abroad to work. Often, when my friends went out at the weekends and stayed out, I would have to go home to cook the evening meal for my father because, bless him, he is not a very good cook (sorry, Dad). Cooking was a necessity but it was something I grew to love. Now, I cannot function if I don't have 'my time' in the kitchen and when I travel for very long periods, I often find myself craving my kitchen – there is only so much eating out one can do, with all the rich food, and it can be too heavy on the body.

When I cook I reconnect with myself and feel sane again. It lifts my spirits and it is as if I am feeding my soul too. If you are an established cook, you will no doubt understand what I mean, but if you are a beginner I hope you will experience that innate pleasure as you start on your cooking journey. I am under no illusion that we all live such stressful lives, juggling work and family life with little time to cook, so I hope that these recipes will come in handy when you need to keep an eye on the clock and base your food decisions around the time available. But if you find yourself with more time on hand, I have also included some dishes that you can really plough your love and attention into with reckless abandon!

Many of the recipes in this book are inspired by Chinese classics and some have been handed down from my family. I am proud to be able to share many of my late grandmother's favourites. I took for granted that she would always be here to see me progress through my career and I am sad that she will not see this book published. I am dedicating this book to her and to her timeless recipes – which will carry me through the rest of my life.

She was my teacher and source of inspiration. My earliest childhood food memory is of sitting on her knee while she worked tirelessly and happily wrapping hundreds of parcels of meaty-rice dumplings to share with all her family and friends (nearly a hundred of them) for the Dragon Boat festival in Taiwan. She was an incredible woman: beautiful, strong and vocal (when she didn't get her way with my grandfather). She was an extremely talented cook who could always whip up something to be on the table in a matter of minutes. But she was also hard to please, with high standards. Whenever I cooked for her, I always expected the criticism, and so the few compliments came as delicious surprises.

Her lessons have been invaluable, from watching her gutting fish and killing live birds, to picking vegetables and rinsing her large wok on the wooden stove ... she groomed me to be a cook without realising. All the visual sights and smells of her traditional Chinese kitchen are always there in my mind when I am cooking and those years were the happiest of my life; of course, I took them for granted because I was a child. She showered us with love through her cooking, through the time she took to prepare all those delicious dishes for us – the labour of her love.

I never knew I would grow up to be a cook and that it would become my career. Many of the memories I have of my life experiences are referenced by food and it always amazes me how dishes, tastes and smells can bring to mind some of the oldest memories lost through time. I will never forget the first time my grandmother came to England. I had the pleasure of cooking for her during her stay and she didn't say anything throughout the trip, but, when she returned to Taiwan, she called me and said she thought my food was delicious. I was so happy.

At a glance – the inspiration behind the dishes

The recipes in this book are wide-ranging, varied and some of my favourites; many of them are versatile and so you can use your imagination and turn them into your own creations.

Throughout the book I've added short cuts and tips to help you save time and I have also included preparation and cooking times and suggested marinating times. For marinades, sometimes I have the forethought to do this overnight, but most often, in a hurry, I will marinate for just 10–20 minutes, depending on how impatient I am to have my meal. So don't feel you have to slavishly marinate for 12 hours if you are pushed for time. Also, some people cook more quickly than others and therefore the guidance times in this book are designed to help with planning and not act as a pressure cooker! So please relax, enjoy and remember, as always, practice makes perfect.

If you are new to Chinese cooking, I would recommend trying some of my quick home-style dishes such as the Shrimp, crabmeat, dofu and spinach soup, which can be turned into a light meal, or my one-wok Chicken, smoky bacon and bamboo shoot stir-fry. My grandmother used to cook dishes such as the Pork with Chinese cabbage and Sichuan stir-fried pork with cucumbers, served with egg-fried rice, and so whenever I cook these I think of her.

One of my favourite quick home meals has to be Saucy pork and tomato egg stir-fry – the sauce is so delicious you can mop it up with plain jasmine rice; this gets the thumbs up with children too and it's a great way of getting them to eat some vegetables. The Saucy beef dofu, Spicy

chunky lamb, and Garlic chilli pepper beef and mushroom pak choy are my family favourites and if you are a fan of noodles then I highly recommend the Rice wine pepper beef noodles. If I am cooking a range of dishes to share, I like to serve Sweetcorn, egg and spring onion stir-fry or Garlic spinach from the vegetarian and side dishes chapter, which both make delicious simple accompaniments.

For those of you after something light and healthy, please do check out my Grandfather's egg, mixed mushroom and celery broth – it may not instantly grab your attention but it is perfect if you are in search of nutrients and something settling on the stomach.

If like me, you are a chilli fanatic, I have included many dishes that will not disappoint and are certainly not for the fainthearted. It is incredibly hard to highlight just a few of those here because I love them all, but Chongqing beef is mind-blowingly delicious and was inspired by a meal I had at a top-class restaurant, 'Hutongs', in Hong Kong. The aromas and flavours are explosive. The Roast beef in 'four-spiced' chilli oil is one that I created when I had some roast beef left over after Sunday lunch but didn't have many fresh ingredients left in the fridge, so I improvised with store cupboard spices and ingredients to make this incredible super quick and tasty dish. It's an impressive dish to serve to important guests because it looks beautifully elegant on the plate (however, do first check that your guests like spicy food!). The Spicy Sichuan pepper prawn-fried rice is my ultimate favourite quick one-wok meal after work; it tastes really good with its large, juicy, fresh tiger prawns. My advice with all these spicy dishes is to make sure you have plenty of water to hand.

If you fancy some of your favourite Chinese takeaway dishes, don't reach for the phone – it's quicker, easier and healthier to cook those dishes at home and I've included lots of recipes for you to try. My reliable and delicious Chicken and black bean stir-fry can be made in only 15 minutes, and to make this dish even quicker get the rice cooking first! You won't find my Sweet and sour duck on your local takeaway menu, it's zesty and full of flavour, while my Juicy chilli chicken and cashew nut is fresher, healthier and tastier that any takeaway dish; just serve this with steamed rice for an addictively tasty midweek supper. When I want something lighter, my curled-up-in-front-of-the-telly Crabmeat sweetcorn soup (with a few shavings of nutty black truffle on top) always hits the spot.

I like to vary my evening meals during the week. In a typical week, I will eat about one vegetarian-themed, two meat and three or four fish or seafood suppers, (because I love fish and seafood). When I was growing up in Southern Taiwan, we lived really close to the port of Kaosiung and I would watch the best fish catches arriving at the local fish markets. In the village where my grandmother lived, old ladies on bicycles would carry small buckets of river fish in water to sell and I can still hear them calling out for customers. The fish and seafood was always fresh and very simply cooked – often steamed, which is one of my favourite ways to cook fish. The fish dish I love the most in this book is the Steamed wine sea bass, but if you like your fish fried I would suggest the Spicy bacon crispy haddock, which is really more-ish and cooks in just 13 minutes. For a more traditional Chinese flavour I recommend the Sweet and smoky 'hong sao yu' (red-cooked fish).

Traditionally, when Chinese entertain they would have something cooking in the oven, steamer and rice-cooker, with a few woks also on the go – because the idea is to have all the dishes shared at the table and therefore served at the same time, which can be extremely stressful for the host! The trick is to prepare some dishes in advance – perhaps a few cold meats like Red-cooked pork or Sichuan chilli roast beef, or 'liang cai' (cold dishes) that you can serve first. Marinades can be made in advance, as can dumplings, so all you have to do is cook them in the steamer and not have to worry about them.

Living and entertaining in the UK means that I have become more accustomed to the Western style of entertaining and so my meals are simpler and mostly with set courses, rather than with all the dishes served at once as in the Chinese style. However, when I have four or fewer guests, I like 'going to town' and I will make a variety of dishes but in smaller portions – more in line with dim sum. For larger groups I tend to make buffet-style dishes so that everyone can help themselves. There is a chapter devoted to recipes for entertaining, but there are plenty of dishes in the other chapters too that would work just as well for entertaining and allow you to cook Chinese but in a Western setting – so you could choose to cook a starter, main and dessert. The dishes I have chosen for the entertaining chapter are popular and easy ones for large crowds, where the ingredients can be doubled or quadrupled in quantity. When you do have a little more time, there are

dishes such as Sichuan spicy pork and prawn wontons in Sichuan chilli oil, Duck spring rolls, and Pork and water chestnut dumplings, for those who love to make things from scratch. Wontons and dumplings can always be made ahead and frozen until you need them. Dishes such as Yellow bean and honey roast chicken may surprise you. It was inspired by my love of British roast dinners ever since I had my first one (teamed with a large Yorkshire pudding) at school and so I couldn't resist including it. It's made with my favourite Chinese spice – Sichuan peppercorns. A special note on the Hainanese chicken rice in this chapter – it may take some time and love but it is delightfully delicious and one of my favourite traditional classic Chinese dishes.

On the subject of classics, I have included some that I cannot live without, such as Century duck eggs with coriander and mushroom sauce – a word of advice: these are only for true Chinese food connoisseurs and take some getting used to, but I love them, pungent and more-ish! I have to mention also my grandmother's Chicken rice 'Bi-ge', a celebration dish that is usually eaten on the Winter Solstice. I love this dish so much that whenever I stayed with my grandmother, I always asked her to make it for me, it is that good. As is my mother's Taiwanese ginger and sesame chicken noodle soup, which will sort out a cold in no time!

Finally, just a quick mention on desserts. The British palate is not quite accustomed to Chinese desserts and I must admit there are a few that do take some getting used to. However, I also know that tastes are changing so for those who are adventurous and after the more traditional Chinese flavours, I have included one of my favourite classic desserts – Tang yuan. It is a sweetened red bean soup that takes me back to China and my childhood and one that I love when it is served hot after a meal. If traditional Chinese desserts are not your thing, then I have also created some 'fu-sian' desserts, such as Lychee and strawberry spring rolls with vanilla ice cream and golden syrup – it can be made in about 18 minutes and is utterly delicious.

No time and money? Chinese food is the answer

One of the most important tips I can offer in cooking is to choose the freshest ingredients possible. The secret to making a dish relies seventy percent on the freshness and quality of the ingredients and thirty percent on your skill. With practice and in time skill can be perfected, but the dish is only as good as the ingredients you start off with.

The best part of making room in your life for cooking Chinese is that it is quick and inexpensive to prepare a delicious healthy meal. The trick to cooking

Chinese at home is to make sure you invest in a good range of Chinese condiments for your store cupboard – essentials such as groundnut oil, light soy sauce, dark soy sauce, dried chilli flakes, Shaohsing rice wine (or dry sherry), toasted sesame oil, rice vinegar, chilli bean sauce, five-spice powder, Sichuan peppercorns and chilli sauce. Once you've bought these essentials it's just a question of buying fresh meat or fish and vegetables and the all-important Chinese flavourings of garlic, ginger and fresh chillies to create some wonderful flavour combinations such as hot-sour, sweet-sour, spicy-sour, savoury-sweet, smoky-sweet and so on. This means that every shopping trip is relatively inexpensive as the condiments last for ages. If you don't have access to a Chinese supermarket, do try to find the authentic ingredients – there are lots of stores online, which help make ordering easier – it is worth the effort because you will taste the difference in your dishes.

Cooking on a wok is fast and fun, and the results are fabulous – so, even if you are starting out, you cannot go wrong with cooking a stir-fry in a wok. Be sure to invest in a good wok; it doesn't need to be expensive and, as long as you look after it, it should last for ages. With my kind of cooking, a good wok and a few utensils are all you need to get going. I've included tips on how to buy, look after and use a wok on pages xiii–xvi.

Of course, there are more intermediate and complex Chinese dishes but, in general, if you are short of time and money, cooking Chinese at home is the answer and it will be tastier, cheaper and much better for you than buying ready-made meals because you will know exactly what you have put into each dish.

Final advice – make time

My advice for everyone is to take your time and enjoy the process of cooking and sharing food with your loved ones – each dish you create may not last long on the plate (or palate) but happy memories will be created that will last forever. Don't be a slave to time, it is there for you to cherish and use, in the present.

These recipes are what I like to cook at home and I have become quite reliant on some of them to keep me balanced. So I really hope you will enjoy cooking and eating them as much as I have enjoyed developing them. I would like to keep bringing delicious food to your table. Sometimes we forget what makes us happy – I hope that some of the dishes I have created will make you happy. With happy blessings and wishes,

Buying & caring for your wok

There is nothing more traditional in Chinese cooking than using the wok. This great invention has been used for centuries to help feed millions of people all over the world.

Woks come in various sizes and are made from different materials, and so when you come to buy one it can be rather challenging. Traditional cast-iron woks are quite heavy and require seasoning, which is not too difficult. The wok comes coated with a film of oil; wash this off using a sponge and washing up liquid, then dry the wok over a high flame on the stove. Next, add a little oil to the wok (sesame oil is good because it burns quickly) and then use absorbent kitchen paper to rub in the oil over the entire wok, giving it a darkened blackened effect. Once your wok is seasoned, don't use a metal scourer or iron wool on it, as you will take off the seasoning.

For those who prefer a lighter wok, I would recommend one made from carbon steel, which you season in the same way as the cast-iron wok. If you are short of time, like me, buy a non-stick wok made from carbon steel – it will require less oil for cooking than a cast-iron wok, so is healthier, too.

When choosing your wok, make sure it feels comfortable and right for you. I prefer a one-handled wok with a medium handle that is not too thick to hold. In terms of size, choose a medium wok, between 30.5cm/12 inches and 40.5cm/16 inches in diameter, which will hold a medium-sized bamboo steamer comfortably and allow you to cook enough to serve at least four.

For those who don't have a gas stove, I would say invest in a new cooker! I find that electric stoves are just not right for wok cooking – you can buy a flat-bottomed wok, but you never really get enough heat to cook the food. However, you could invest in a good electric wok, which I have used before and found not too bad.

Techniques for cooking in a wok

Stir-frying

The classic use for a wok – a touch of oil and lots of stirring ensure that the ingredients keep their crunch and take on a smoky flavour. To help you cook your dish to perfection, however, there are some things to observe.

1 Preparation

Do prepare all the ingredients in advance, because once you start cooking, you won't have time to stop and start chopping. Cut all the meat or fish to the same size – this ensures that the pieces cook in the same time. This principle also applies to vegetables. For leafy vegetables, cut them on the diagonal – this exposes them to more heat in the wok and they will cook more rapidly.

2 Choosing the right oil

Most oils with a high heating point can be used, such as sunflower oil, groundnut oil and vegetable oil, but avoid sesame oil as this has a low heating point and burns quickly – use it for seasoning your dishes. Olive oil isn't ideal because its flavour does not suit all Chinese dishes. It is best to use flavourless oil. My favourite is groundnut – it has a slight nutty aroma that is not strong enough to overpower a dish, but acts as a great base on which to create the layers of flavours.

3 The correct heat

To prepare the wok for stir-frying, heat it to a high heat, then add the oil and swirl it around in the wok. When the wok starts to smoke it's ready to use.

   During the cooking process, keep an eye on the flame and level of heat in the wok both before and after adding the food – the temperature in the wok will fall once the ingredients have been added so you want the heat high enough to sear the food, but not so high that you burn the ingredients.

4 Adding raw ingredients and timing

The ingredients should go into the wok in the following order. Add the Chinese essentials such as garlic, ginger and chillies first. Secondly, add the meat or seafood, and then, lastly, the vegetables, with a sprinkling of water to create steam. This order of cooking helps to retain the bite of the vegetables. It is important to dry the ingredients before you add them to the wok or the oil will spit, and if there is too much moisture the ingredients will stew rather than 'fry'. If you are using sauces or meats marinated in sauces, don't add the sauce or marinade until the end of the stir-frying process to ensure it doesn't all evaporate, and to prevent stewing the food.

Sometimes the meat/protein is cooked and then removed from the wok while the vegetables are stir-fried. It is then returned to the wok for the final mixing with seasoning. I find that you don't always have to cook in this way (as recipes vary), and there are some dishes where you can add the meat/protein after the garlic, ginger and chillies and then, once they start to cook, you can add the rest of the ingredients; this helps to ensure the meat/protein is not overly cooked.

5 Adding cooked ingredients

Cooked noodles or cooked rice can be added to the wok at the end of the cooking process and combined with the rest of the ingredients together with all the seasoning.

Steaming

Food cooked in a bamboo steamer takes on a subtle bamboo fragrance. This technique is a wonderful way of preparing a healthy meal; it's fast and fun, too. You can also serve your food in the steamer, with the lid on; this helps to keep the food warm for longer.

1 Make sure the wok is stable

If you are cooking on a gas stove, invest in a wok rest; this helps to keep the wok secure.

2 Filling the wok with water

Fill the wok half full with water and place the bamboo steamer over the top, making sure the water in the wok does not touch the base of the steamer. Depending on the recipe, either place the food to be steamed directly in the steamer or on a heatproof plate, bowl or rack that fits inside the steamer, raised above the water. Put the lid on and steam. If necessary, top up the wok with more boiling water as the food cooks.

3 Size of the bamboo steamer

Bamboo steamers vary in size, so make sure that you buy one that sits snugly across the wok and will not touch the water when this is added. For those who love to cook a feast, you can pile the steamers on as high as you want (although you will need a powerful flame that can produce enough steam to reach the highest steamer; I would say up to three piled high should be okay).

4 A final tip

Before you attempt to take the lid off the steamer, make sure that you always turn the flame off under the wok. I have been impatient many times and have burnt my hands and arms in the hot steam.

Deep-frying

You might think this not a very healthy way of cooking, but if the oil is hot enough, once the food is dropped in it will cook at such a high temperature that the outside edges are almost 'sealed', not allowing the ingredient to absorb any more oil, and the high heat continues to cook the inside of the food.

1 Make sure the wok is stable

Again, if you are cooking on a gas stove, invest in a wok rest; this helps to keep the wok stable and secure – very important when deep-frying.

2 Make sure the oil is hot enough

To get the best results from deep-frying, make sure you use a deep-frying thermometer and follow the recommended temperature given in the recipe. If the oil is too cold, the food will take longer to cook and the result is oily food. If the temperature is too hot, the food will burn and will be undercooked on the inside. If you don't have a thermometer, then you can use the 'bread test', which I refer to in my recipes. Be particularly careful when deep-frying in a wok – don't overfill it, or leave it unattended.

3 Adding and removing the food

When lowering food into deep oil, I use a utensil called a 'spider'. It is a web-like, woven steel mesh scooper that works well as a strainer. Use it also for lifting fried foods from the wok (draining much oil in the process) onto dishes lined with absorbent kitchen paper (again, to help drain excess oil). The 'spider' comes in different sizes and you should be able to find it in all good Chinese supermarkets and kitchen/cookware shops. It often has a handle made of bamboo.

4 Golden rules when deep-frying

- Make sure the wok is stable, or use a wok stand.
- Do not over-fill the wok with oil – it should be less than half full, when there is less chance of bubbling and spilling over.
- Make sure the food is dry, as this prevents spitting.
- For best results, avoid re-using oil whenever possible.
- Use a large, long pair of bamboo chopsticks to help you turn food over if necessary (not plastic chopsticks, as they melt).
- Serve fried food immediately as it will start to lose its crunch and crispness. However, if unavoidable, keep the food hot in a preheated oven before serving.

Other cooking utensils

The following would also be useful to have in the kitchen:

Wok cover

Invest in a wok cover; this will allow you to stew, steam, boil and smoke food using your wok. It should have a small top handle to allow you to lift it off, and it should fit snug and firm on the wok.

Wok brush

This is a wooden brush with long hard bristles that is used with hot water to clean the wok. It's not essential but can take the hard work out of cleaning.

Chinese spatula /wooden spoon

Traditionally, the metal spatula is used in the Chinese kitchen to allow you to manoeuvre the food and scoop it out of the wok. This is okay for seasoned woks, but you may end up scratching off the non-stick coating if you use a non-stick coated wok. I would suggest a wooden spoon as an alternative.

Ladle

The Chinese ladle is small and bowl-shaped to allow you to collect soups and sauces from the wok, but I use a normal ladle, and not necessarily made from carbon steel as they can rust easily. Mine is made from stainless steel.

Chinese cleaver/good knife

It is essential to invest in a good knife. I usually use a medium stainless steel chef's knife that is made from one continuous piece of metal. However, I also have a stainless steel Chinese cleaver with a wooden handle. Cleavers are particularly useful for hacking meat with bones, such as ribs, chopping up chicken, or chopping through roast duck. They are also useful for slicing, shredding, dicing, mincing and mashing (by using the side of the blade and mashing the ingredient between the blade and the chopping board). Of course, you can use a food processor but I find it is good therapy to use the cleaver.

Cutting board

Choose a solid, large wooden chopping board and make sure you clean it well after use. I usually keep three different boards: one for meat, one for seafood, and one for fruit and vegetables.

Soups & Starters

Traditional-style hot & sour soup	30 minutes (plus 20 minutes soaking)
Sea bass & dofu clear soup	30 minutes (plus 20 minutes soaking)
Grandma's pork & golden needle soup	25 minutes (plus 20 minutes soaking)
Crabmeat sweetcorn soup with black truffle	20 minutes
Shrimp, crabmeat, dofu & spinach soup	15 minutes
Grandfather's egg, mixed mushroom & celery broth	15 minutes
Yellow bean scallops & chives	20 minutes (plus 10 minutes marinating)
Wok-fried crispy scallops	30 minutes
Butter batter prawns	22 minutes
Century duck eggs with coriander & mushroom sauce	5 minutes
Sweet & sour Wuxi ribs	15 minutes (plus 20 minutes marinating)

Traditional-style hot & sour soup

This is warming on a cold winter's day and is delightfully crunchy, full of texture and flavour. To turn this into a snack, add more stock and some pre-soaked rice noodles before seasoning.

SERVES 4

- 1 litre/1¾ pints water
- 1 tablespoon vegetable bouillon powder or stock powder
- 1 tablespoon freshly grated root ginger
- 2 medium red chillies, deseeded and finely chopped
- 300g/11oz cooked chicken breast, shredded
- 1 teaspoon Shaohsing rice wine or dry sherry
- 2 tablespoons dark soy sauce
- 1 x 220g tin of bamboo shoots, drained
- 10g dried wood ear mushrooms, pre-soaked in hot water for 20 minutes, then drained and finely sliced

- 100g/3½oz fresh firm dofu (bean curd), cut into 5cm/2 inch long x 1cm/ ½ inch wide strips
- 50g/2oz Sichuan preserved vegetables, rinsed and sliced, or pickled cornichons with a little fresh chopped chilli added
- 2 tablespoons light soy sauce
- 3 tablespoons Chinkiang black rice vinegar or balsamic vinegar
- 1 tablespoon chilli oil
- a few pinches of ground white pepper
- 1 egg, lightly beaten
- 1 tablespoon cornflour blended with 2 tablespoons cold water
- 1 large spring onion, finely sliced
- freshly chopped coriander to garnish (optional)

1 Pour the water into a pan and bring to the boil. Add the bouillon powder and stir to dissolve. Bring back to the boil, then add all the ingredients up to and including the wood ear mushrooms. Turn the heat down to medium, then add the dofu, Sichuan vegetables or cornichons, soy sauce, vinegar, chilli oil and white pepper and simmer for 10 minutes.

2 Stir in the egg, then add the blended cornflour and stir to thicken the soup (add more if you like a thicker consistency).

3 Add the spring onion, garnish with coriander, if you like, and serve immediately.

Ching's Tip

■ You can vary this recipe to your taste and adjust the amount of chillies to your preference. You could also omit the chicken strips if you are vegetarian. My mother changes it all the time by adding different Chinese leaves.

Sea bass & dofu clear soup

Fish is so quick to cook and this broth makes a delicious, comforting and nutritious dinner. It can be served as a starter or as a main if you're after something light.

**SERVES 2 AS A MAIN OR
4 AS A STARTER**

about 250g/9oz sea bass fillets (skin on),
  each fillet cut into 4 pieces (you can
  ask the fishmonger to do all this)

800ml/1 pint 7fl oz water

2.5cm/1 inch piece of fresh root
  ginger, peeled and sliced

1 tablespoon Shaohsing rice wine
  or dry sherry

3 dried Chinese mushrooms,
  pre-soaked in hot water for
  20 minutes, then drained and sliced

1 tablespoon dried shrimps, pre-soaked
  in hot water for 20 minutes, then
  drained

3 large spring onions, sliced at an
  angle into 5cm/2 inch strips

200g/7oz fresh firm dofu (bean curd),
  cut into 1.5cm/⅔ inch squares

1 teaspoon vegetable bouillon
  powder or stock powder

a dash of toasted sesame oil

salt and ground white pepper

finely chopped fresh coriander
  to serve (optional)

1 Rinse the fish in cold running water and pat dry with absorbent kitchen paper. Pour the water into a pan or wok and bring to the boil. Add the fish and all the ingredients up to and including the dofu. Turn the heat down to medium and cook for 15 minutes, or until the fish is cooked and the dofu has absorbed all the flavours in the broth.

2 Season with the bouillon powder and salt and white pepper to taste and add a dash of toasted sesame oil. Garnish with chopped coriander, if you like, and serve immediately.

Prep time: 5 minutes, cook in: 20 minutes
(plus 20 minutes soaking)

Grandma's pork & golden needle soup

My grandmother was the best cook in our family, incredibly creative and inspiring, and she used to make a soup similar to this, quite often with the addition of crunchy freshly boiled and sliced bamboo shoots.

SERVES 4

1 tablespoon groundnut oil

2cm/¾ inch piece of fresh root ginger, peeled and sliced

6 large pork spare ribs, each cut into thirds and rinsed in cold water

1 tablespoon Shaohsing rice wine or dry sherry

1 small carrot, diced

2 ripe red tomatoes, sliced and any hard centres discarded

1 litre/1¾ pints water

1 tablespoon vegetable bouillon powder or stock powder

40g/1½oz golden needles (dried lily flowers), pre-soaked in hot water for 20 minutes, then drained, or 75g/3oz tinned bamboo shoots

1 tablespoon light soy sauce

1 teaspoon toasted sesame oil

1 pinch of ground white pepper

1 Heat a pan over a medium heat and add the groundnut oil. When the oil starts to smoke, add the ginger and stir-fry for a few seconds, then add the pork ribs and stir-fry for 2 minutes until browned. As the ribs start to turn brown, add the rice wine or sherry.

2 Add the carrot, tomatoes and water and stir in the bouillon powder. Simmer, uncovered, on a medium heat for 10 minutes, skimming off any scum on the surface of the soup as necessary.

3 Add the golden needles or bamboo shoots and simmer for 5 minutes. Season with the soy sauce, sesame oil and white pepper and then serve immediately.

Ching's Tip

■ Golden needles are also known as dried lily flowers and you can buy them from Chinese supermarkets or online. They impart an earthy sweet flavour and their stems provide a satisfying slightly crunchy texture. If you can't get hold of them, use tinned bamboo shoots instead.

Prep time: 5 minutes,
cook in: 15 minutes

Crabmeat sweetcorn soup with black truffle

Really quick and easy to make, this soup can be dished up in minutes and is the perfect weekday supper, served with a brown bread roll and butter.

SERVES 4

1 litre/1¾ pints water

2 x 170g tins of crabmeat in brine

2 x 200g tins of sweetcorn, drained

1 large ripe red tomato, sliced

2 eggs, beaten

3 tablespoons light soy sauce

1 tablespoon sesame oil

2 tablespoons cornflour blended with 4 tablespoons cold water

1 large spring onion, sliced

sea salt and ground white pepper

Chinese black truffle to serve (optional)

1 Pour the water into a large pan and bring to the boil. Add the crabmeat, sweetcorn and tomato, turn the heat down and simmer for 5 minutes.

2 Add the beaten eggs and stir gently to create a web-like pattern in the soup, as the egg whites and yolks start to cook. Season with the soy sauce, sesame oil, salt and white pepper, adding more to taste as necessary. Bring to the boil, then stir in the blended cornflour to thicken the soup. Turn the heat down, sprinkle in the spring onion and simmer on a gentle heat until ready to serve.

3 Ladle the soup into serving bowls, grate some black truffle over the top, if you like, and enjoy!

Ching's Tip

■ You can dress this dish up to serve at a dinner party by adding fresh crab or lobster meat.

Shrimp, crabmeat, dofu & spinach soup

Very quick, very simple, this is a delicious soup that is also very nutritious. Make sure you use a good-quality vegetable or fish stock.

SERVES 2 AS A MAIN OR 4 AS A STARTER

700ml/1 pint 3½fl oz fish stock or vegetable stock

200g/7oz shrimps

200g/7oz fresh firm dofu (bean curd), cut into 1cm/½ inch cubes

1 x 170g tin of crabmeat in brine

150g/5oz spinach

1 egg, beaten

1 tablespoon light soy sauce

a dash of toasted sesame oil

sea salt and ground white pepper

1 spring onion, finely sliced to garnish

1 Heat a pan, add the stock and bring to the boil. Add the shrimps, dofu and crabmeat and stir well, then turn the heat down to a simmer and cook for 2 minutes.

2 Add the spinach, egg, soy sauce, sesame oil, salt and pepper and stir well. Garnish with the spring onion and serve.

Grandfather's egg, mixed mushroom & celery broth

This is one of my grandfather's favourite soups – nourishing, comforting and healthy, it is also quick to make. The shiitake mushrooms impart a smoky, earthy flavour, but you can use any mushrooms you like.

SERVES 4

1 litre/1¾ pints water

2 celery stalks, finely diced

2 eggs, beaten

1 teaspoon vegetable bouillon
   powder or stock powder

60g/2½oz shiitake mushrooms

125g/4oz mixed oyster
   mushrooms

1 tablespoon light soy sauce

a dash of toasted sesame oil

sea salt and ground white pepper

1 Pour the water into a pan and bring to the boil. Add the celery and cook for 2 minutes, then add the beaten eggs and stir gently to create a web-like pattern in the broth, as the egg whites and yolks start to cook.

2 Turn the heat down to medium, add the bouillon powder and all the mushrooms and simmer gently for 2 minutes. Season to taste with the soy sauce, sesame oil, salt and white pepper and serve immediately.

Ching's Tip

■ For a slightly thicker soup, you can add some cornflour blended with water to the simmering broth at the end of the seasoning step, if you like.

Yellow bean scallops & chives

This is an elegant and easy starter to make. The key is to buy fresh, juicy scallops, they make all the difference to the texture and flavour.

SERVES 2 AS A MAIN OR 4 TO SHARE

12 raw scallops on the shell
1 tablespoon groundnut oil
finely chopped chives to garnish
mixed salad leaves to serve

FOR THE PASTE

1 tablespoon yellow bean paste
  (see Ching's Tips)
1 teaspoon freshly grated root
  ginger
1 pinch of brown sugar
1 tablespoon Shaohsing rice wine
  or dry sherry
1 teaspoon light soy sauce
1 teaspoon dark soy sauce
1 teaspoon clear rice vinegar or
  cider vinegar

1 Remove the scallops from their shells, then remove and discard the hard muscle on the side. Leave the coral on, if you like, or remove it. Trim and rinse the scallops and pat dry.

2 Put all the ingredients for the paste into a bowl and mix well. Place the scallops in the paste and leave to marinate for 10 minutes.

3 Heat a wok over a high heat and add the groundnut oil. When the oil starts to smoke, add the scallops (retaining the marinade) and cook for 1 minute, then toss the wok to turn the scallops and cook for a further 1 minute. Transfer the scallops onto a serving plate.

4 Add the reserved marinade to the wok and cook until thick and slightly sticky. Pour over the scallops, garnish with the chives and serve with mixed salad leaves.

Ching's Tips

- Yellow bean paste is made from salted yellow beans that have been preserved in salt, spices and sometimes chilli too. You can also buy fermented whole yellow beans (soya beans), then blitz them in a blender and add your own spices to make a paste.
- This dish is also delicious served with a small portion of the Spicy Wild Rice Salad on page 146, and washed down with a glass of cold bubbly.

Wok-fried crispy scallops

This is one of my favourite starters to serve when I have VIP guests!
It is quick to make and tastes wonderful. The crunchy-crisp topping
with the tender scallops is a delight.

SERVES 2

10 raw scallops on the shell

1 tablespoon groundnut oil

½ teaspoon Sichuan peppercorns

1 tablespoon Shaohsing rice wine
   or dry sherry

1 teaspoon light soy sauce

1 pinch of brown sugar

½ lemon

1 medium red chilli, deseeded
   and finely chopped

2 tablespoons vegetable stock

mixed fresh herbs to garnish

mixed salad leaves to serve

FOR THE CRISPY 'SEAWEED' AND CRISPY LEEK

1 small baby leek, diced and
   dried thoroughly

potato flour or cornflour

300ml/10fl oz groundnut oil

1 head of green pak choy, leaf
   part only, finely shredded
   and dried thoroughly

coarse sea salt

light brown sugar

1 First make the crispy 'seaweed' and leek. Lightly coat the leek in potato flour or cornflour (no need to coat the pak choy). Heat the groundnut oil in a large pan to 180°C/350°F or until a cube of bread dropped in turns golden brown in 15 seconds and floats to the surface. Using a slotted spoon, lower the leek and pak choy pieces into the oil and deep-fry for 5 minutes until they turn golden brown. Lift out and drain on absorbent kitchen paper, then add some sea salt and brown sugar and toss gently with your fingers so the seasoning lightly coats the crispy 'seaweed' and leek.

2 Remove the scallops from their shells, then remove and discard the hard muscle on the side. Leave the coral on, if you like, or remove it. Trim and rinse the scallops and pat dry.

3 Heat a wok over a high heat and add the groundnut oil, then add the Sichuan peppercorns and heat for a few seconds to release their aroma. Add the scallops to the wok and leave to settle for 1 minute, then toss the wok and the scallops. As the scallops start to turn opaque, add the rice wine or sherry, followed by the soy sauce. Cook for a further minute, then add the sugar and a squeeze of fresh lemon juice (catch the pips in your hands) and sprinkle the chilli into the wok. Transfer the scallops into a dish. Add the stock to the wok and heat through, then turn off the heat.

4 To serve, put the scallops onto serving plates and drizzle with the remaining juices from the wok. Sprinkle with the crispy garnish and chopped chilli from the wok, dress with fresh mixed herbs and serve immediately with mixed salad leaves.

Ching's Tip

- The crispy 'seaweed' is incredibly easy to make and you can also garnish this dish with some fine mixed Oriental herbs such as shisho and mustard cress for an elegant finish.

Sweet & sour Wuxi ribs

The traditional way of preparing these ribs is to slow-braise them in stock, then add the sauce and thicken with blended cornflour. However, for a quicker dish and richer flavour I have shallow-fried the ribs.

SERVES 2 TO SHARE

600g/1lb 5oz pork ribs, chopped
   into 3–4cm/1¼–1½ inch
   lengths

groundnut oil for shallow-frying

sea salt and ground white pepper

1 spring onion, sliced, to garnish

FOR THE MARINADE

2 garlic cloves, finely chopped

2 tablespoons yellow bean sauce

1 tablespoon Shaohsing rice wine
   or dry sherry

FOR THE SWEET AND SOUR SAUCE

2 tablespoons light soy sauce

2 tablespoons Chinkiang black
   rice vinegar or balsamic vinegar

1 tablespoon brown sugar

1 tablespoon runny honey

1 Put all the ingredients for the marinade into a large bowl and stir to combine. Add the pork ribs and turn to coat, then cover the bowl and leave to marinate for at least 20 minutes, or as long as possible, in the fridge.

2 Heat a wok over a high heat. Fill the wok to a quarter of its depth with groundnut oil and heat the oil to 180°C/350°F or until a cube of bread dropped in turns golden brown in 15 seconds. Using a spider, carefully add the ribs and shallow-fry until browned.

3 Meanwhile, put all the ingredients for the sweet and sour sauce into a small bowl and stir to combine.

4 Lift the ribs out of the wok with the spider and drain on absorbent kitchen paper. Drain the wok of oil and wipe it clean, then reheat over a high heat.

5 Add the ribs and sauce mixture to the wok and cook on a low–medium heat for 5–6 minutes until the sauce has reduced to a sticky and thicker consistency. Season further to taste with salt and white pepper, garnish with the spring onion and serve immediately.

Pork

Pork with Chinese leaf — 15 minutes (plus 20 minutes marinating)

Sichuan stir-fried pork with cucumbers — 10 minutes (plus 20 minutes marinating)

Fried pork cutlet — 15 minutes (plus 20 minutes marinating)

Cantonese-style sweet & sour pork — 15 minutes

Saucy pork & tomato egg stir-fry — 15 minutes

Red-cooked pork — 50 minutes

Griddled honey yellow bean pork — 25 minutes (plus 20 minutes marinating)

Crispy twice-cooked pork — 25 minutes

Prep time: 10 minutes, cook in: 5 minutes
(plus 20 minutes marinating)

Pork with Chinese leaf

Chinese leaf has crinkled pale green leaves and a white crunchy stem. It makes a simple but delicious meal when served with egg-fried rice.

SERVES 2

300g/11oz pork fillet, sliced widthways and then cut into lengthways strips

1 tablespoon yellow bean sauce

2 tablespoons potato flour or cornflour

3 tablespoons groundnut oil

1 tablespoon Shaohsing rice wine or dry sherry

1 garlic clove, finely chopped

1 red chilli, deseeded and finely chopped

150g/5oz Chinese leaf, cut into chunks

1–2 tablespoons light soy sauce

1 teaspoon toasted sesame oil

egg-fried rice to serve (see page 155)

1 Put the pork into a bowl, add the yellow bean sauce and stir to coat the meat. Cover the bowl and leave to marinate for at least 20 minutes, or overnight if possible, in the fridge.

2 Just before cooking, coat the meat in the potato flour or cornflour.

3 Heat a wok or pan over a high heat, then add the groundnut oil. When the oil starts to smoke, add the pork and cook for 1 minute. Add the rice wine or sherry and stir-fry for 2 minutes, then add the garlic, chilli and Chinese leaf and stir well.

4 Season with the soy sauce and sesame oil and serve immediately with egg-fried rice.

Ching's Tips

- While the pork is marinating, you can be getting on with the rest of the meal.
- This is also a good dish to share, with other dishes, at a dinner party.

Sichuan stir-fried pork with cucumbers

This easy stir-fry reminds me of my grandmother's cooking – simple but full of flavour. It makes a fast and delicious supper.

SERVES 2

1 tablespoon chilli bean sauce
(or to taste)

300g/11oz pork fillet, sliced
widthways and then cut into
lengthways strips

2 tablespoons potato flour or
cornflour

3–4 tablespoons groundnut oil

1 tablespoon Sichuan
peppercorns

½ tablespoon Shaohsing rice
wine or dry sherry

1 tablespoon light soy sauce

1 tablespoon Chinkiang black rice
vinegar or balsamic vinegar

1 teaspoon toasted sesame oil

1 cucumber, peeled and sliced
lengthways into thin strips
(using a potato peeler)

steamed jasmine rice to serve
(see page 154)

1 Put the chilli bean sauce into a bowl, add the pork
and turn to coat, then cover the bowl and leave to
marinate for 20 minutes, or overnight if possible,
in the fridge.

2 Just before cooking, coat the meat in potato flour
or cornflour.

3 Heat a wok or pan over a high heat, then add the
groundnut oil. When the oil starts to smoke, add
the Sichuan peppercorns, stirring quickly to avoid
burning them. After a few seconds, add the pork strips
and stir together. As the pork starts to cook, add the
rice wine or sherry and stir-fry for 1 minute.

4 Season the pork with soy sauce, vinegar and sesame
oil. Add the cucumber slices and stir well. Serve
immediately with jasmine rice.

Prep time: 5 minutes, cook in: 10 minutes
(plus 20 minutes marinating)

Fried pork cutlet

Fried pork cutlet, or Zha Pai Gu, is crispy and full of flavour. Serve with a refreshing pickled cucumber salad and rice.

SERVES 2

2 x 175g/6oz boneless pork loin
    chops

groundnut oil for deep-frying

3 tablespoons potato flour
    or cornflour

1 egg, beaten

8 tablespoons Panko
    breadcrumbs or stale
    white breadcrumbs

pickled cucumber salad, stir-fried
    vegetables and plain rice
    to serve

FOR THE MARINADE

3 garlic cloves, finely chopped

1 tablespoon light soy sauce

1 tablespoon Shaohsing rice
    wine or dry sherry

1 tablespoon yellow bean sauce

2.5cm/1 inch piece of fresh root
    ginger, peeled and sliced

1 pinch of sugar

1 Flatten the pork loins with a meat cleaver, meat hammer or rolling pin until they are 1cm/½ inch thick. Put all the ingredients for the marinade into a bowl and stir to combine. Add the pork and turn to coat, then cover the bowl and leave to marinate for 20 minutes.

2 Heat a wok over a high heat, then fill the wok to one-third of its depth with groundnut oil. Heat the oil to 180°C/350°F or until a cube of bread dropped in turns golden brown in 15 seconds and floats to the surface.

3 Remove each piece of pork from the marinade, dip in the potato flour or cornflour, then in the beaten egg and cover in the breadcrumbs. Using a pair of tongs or long bamboo chopsticks, carefully lower each piece into the oil and fry for 5–6 minutes until golden brown. Serve immediately with pickled cucumber salad, stir-fried vegetables and rice.

Ching's Tip

■ Many cities of Taiwan have small outlets serving 'Pian-tung', meaning 'convenient lunchboxes' – polystyrene boxes packed with rice, soy-braised seaweed, soy egg, pickled vegetables and stir-fried spinach with a choice of fried fish (swordfish or tuna, and so on). My favourite is the works with a large portion of fried pork cutlet.

Cantonese-style sweet & sour pork

You will recognise this sweet and sour pork recipe as similar to those that are served in the Chinese restaurants in the UK. This is my super-quick, healthier and lighter version.

SERVES 2 AS A MAIN OR 4 TO SHARE

1 egg, beaten

1 tablespoon cornflour

250g/9oz pork fillet, cut into 5mm/¼ inch slices

groundnut oil for deep-frying

1 tablespoon freshly grated root ginger

1 red pepper, deseeded and cut into chunks

1 green pepper, deseeded and cut into chunks

1 x 227g tin of pineapple chunks, sliced and juice retained

1 tablespoon light soy sauce

1 tablespoon clear rice vinegar or cider vinegar

½ teaspoon brown sugar (optional)

1 teaspoon cornflour blended with 1 tablespoon cold water

sea salt and ground white pepper

egg-fried rice to serve (see page 155)

1 Put the egg and cornflour into a bowl and mix to create a batter. Place the pork slices in the mixture and season with salt and white pepper.

2 Heat a wok over a high heat, then fill the wok to one-third of its depth with groundnut oil. Heat until the oil glistens and when a small piece of bread dropped in turns golden brown in 15 seconds and floats to the surface. Using a spider or slotted spoon, carefully add the pork to the oil and fry for 3–4 minutes until golden brown. Lift out using the spider or spoon and drain on absorbent kitchen paper.

3 Pour the oil from the wok through a sieve into a heatproof container and save to use later. Return 1 tablespoon oil to the wok and heat until smoking, then add the ginger and pepper chunks and quickly stir in to stop the ginger from catching. Stir-fry for 2 minutes, then add the pineapple and its juice and bring to the bubble over a high heat. Season with soy sauce, vinegar and brown sugar, if using. Then, as the liquid in the wok reduces and boils, add the blended cornflour and stir to thicken.

4 Return the pork to the wok, stir and toss together well so the pork is covered in the sauce, then serve with egg-fried rice.

Prep time: 5 minutes,
cook in: 10 minutes

Saucy pork & tomato egg stir-fry

Quick and easy to make, this stir-fry is great for a one-pot supper and it's full of nutrients too.

SERVES 2 AS A MAIN OR 4 TO SHARE

1 tablespoon groundnut oil

4 garlic cloves, finely chopped

2 red chillies, deseeded and finely chopped

500g/1lb 2oz lean minced pork

1 tablespoon Shaohsing rice wine or dry sherry

1 tablespoon dark soy sauce

2 ripe red tomatoes, each sliced into eight

1 x 400g tin of chopped tomatoes

1 red pepper, deseeded and sliced into strips

½ teaspoon dried chilli flakes

1 tablespoon light soy sauce

2 eggs, beaten

2 spring onions, finely sliced

1 tablespoon cornflour blended with 2 tablespoons cold water

steamed jasmine rice to serve (see page 154)

1 Heat a wok over a high heat and add the groundnut oil. When the oil starts to smoke, add the garlic and stir-fry for a few seconds. Add the chillies and stir-fry for a few seconds, then add the pork and stir-fry for 1 minute. As the pork starts to cook, add the rice wine or sherry, the dark soy sauce, all the tomatoes and the red pepper. Turn the heat down to medium and cook for 2 minutes to soften the vegetables.

2 Add the chilli flakes and season with the light soy sauce, or to taste. Bring the ingredients to a gentle bubble, then add the beaten eggs and stir gently to create a web-like pattern in the soup, as the egg whites and yolks start to cook.

3 Stir in the spring onions, then bring the dish to a bubble again. Add the blended cornflour and stir to thicken the sauce. Serve immediately with jasmine rice.

Ching's Tip

■ You can add cooked egg noodles to the wok before the seasoning stage if you prefer. This dish would work well with thick udon noodles too. You can also substitute minced beef for the minced pork, or stir some spinach into the dish ... the possibilities are endless!

Red-cooked pork

A popular favourite during frugal times in China. The pork is traditionally slow-cooked in a soy liquid flavoured with star anise. However, I have been more indulgent with lots of spices and flavours. The 'red' refers to the deep red colour of the cooking liquid.

SERVES 4 TO SHARE

1 litre/1¾ pints water

1 tablespoon Sichuan
    peppercorns

6 star anise

2 large cinnamon sticks

2 red tea bags

2cm/¾ inch piece of fresh root
    ginger, peeled and sliced

5 tablespoons light soy sauce

1 tablespoon dark soy sauce

1 whole dried chilli

50g/2oz rock sugar or
    2–3 tablespoons light
    brown sugar

600g/1lb 5oz pork belly, cut into
    2cm/¾ inch chunks

steamed rice or mashed
    potatoes, and stir-fried
    vegetables to serve

1 Put all the ingredients into a large pan and cook, uncovered, on a medium heat for about 45 minutes until the liquid is reduced by half. Skim off any scum on the surface of the liquid.

2 Remove the tea bags before serving. Serve with steamed rice or mashed potatoes, and stir-fried vegetables.

Griddled honey yellow bean pork

Easy to make, this savoury-sweet dish uses one of my favourite marinades. You could use chicken thighs, wings or drumsticks instead of pork, especially in summer for a delicious barbecue.

SERVES 2 AS A MAIN OR 4 TO SHARE

350g/12oz pork fillet

1 tablespoon groundnut oil

2 garlic cloves, finely chopped

1 medium red chilli, deseeded and finely chopped

200g/7oz pak choy, stems and leaves separated and sliced

sea salt

1 spring onion, sliced, to garnish

Mum's sweet potato jasmine rice to serve (see page 137)

FOR THE MARINADE

3 garlic cloves, finely chopped

1 tablespoon freshly grated root ginger

2 tablespoons yellow bean sauce

2 tablespoons runny honey

2 tablespoons light soy sauce

2 tablespoons Shaohsing rice wine or dry sherry

½ teaspoon dark soy sauce

2 tablespoons groundnut oil

1 teaspoon soft brown sugar

1 Put all the ingredients for the marinade into a bowl and stir to combine. Add the pork and turn to coat, then cover the bowl and leave to marinate for 20 minutes. Preheat the oven to 200°C/400°F/gas mark 6.

2 Heat a griddle pan on a high heat and cook the pork for 2 minutes on each side until the outside edges are glazed and sticky. Retain the marinade.

3 Transfer the pork to a roasting tray and roast in the oven for 12 minutes. Remove from the oven and leave to rest for 10 minutes, then slice. Meanwhile, pour the reserved marinade into the griddle pan and heat up, then leave to one side.

4 Heat a wok over a high heat and add the groundnut oil. When the oil starts to smoke, add the garlic and chilli and stir-fry for a few seconds. Add the stems of the pak choy and stir-fry for 1 minute, then add a small splash of water to help create some steam. Add the pak choy leaves, stir for another minute and season with salt.

5 To serve, place the pak choy on a serving plate. Toss the pork fillet in the hot cooked marinade and place on top of the pak choy. Garnish with the spring onion and serve immediately with sweet potato jasmine rice.

Crispy twice-cooked pork

This is a famous Sichuan dish, 'Hui guo ro'. First the pork is boiled in an aromatic stock, then sliced and fried until crisp, then it is stir-fried with chilli and black bean paste and a host of Chinese seasonings. This is my version.

SERVES 2

300g/11oz pork belly

600ml/1 pint water

1 tablespoon Shaohsing rice wine
   or dry sherry

7.5cm/3 inch piece of fresh root
   ginger, peeled and sliced

2 spring onions, sliced

1 teaspoon ground dry-toasted
   Sichuan peppercorns
   (see Ching's Tips)

cornflour

200ml/7fl oz groundnut oil

5 baby leeks, sliced in half lengthways
   (so that the baby corn, sugar snap
   peas and leeks are all the same
   length)

100g/3½oz baby corn, sliced in half
   lengthways

75g/3oz sugar snap peas

steamed jasmine rice to serve
   (see page 154)

FOR THE SAUCE

1 teaspoon chilli bean paste

1 teaspoon fermented salted black
   beans, washed and crushed

1 tablespoon yellow bean paste

1 tablespoon Shaohsing rice wine or
   dry sherry

1 teaspoon dark soy sauce

1 teaspoon light soy sauce

1 teaspoon Sichuan pepper oil/chilli oil

1 pinch of sugar

1 Put the pork into a large pan with the water, rice wine or sherry, two-thirds of the ginger and all the spring onions. Bring to the boil and boil for 12 minutes, then drain and leave to cool.

2 Slice the pork belly across into thin slices, season with the ground Sichuan peppercorns and dust in cornflour.

3 Heat a wok over a high heat, then add the groundnut oil. Heat the oil to 180°C/350°F or until a cube of bread dropped in turns golden brown in 15 seconds and floats to the surface. Add the pork slices and shallow-fry for 3 minutes or until golden brown. Drain on absorbent kitchen paper.

4 Pour the oil from the wok through a sieve into a heatproof container and save to use later. Return 1 teaspoon oil to the wok and heat. Add the remaining sliced ginger (slice it more finely if necessary) and stir-fry for a few seconds, then add all the ingredients for the sauce and stir well. Return the pork to the wok with the leeks, baby corn and sugar snap peas. Stir well, then stir-fry for 2 minutes until the vegetables are al dente. Serve immediately with jasmine rice.

Ching's Tips

- You can boil and cook batches of the belly pork and freeze until you are ready to use it. Then, once defrosted, it is easy to slice the pork into wafer-thin slices before frying.
- To dry-toast Sichuan peppercorns, place in a small pan and heat until fragrant, then crush them in a spice grinder or pestle and mortar until finely ground (or place in a ziplock bag and smash with a rolling pin).
- For chilli lovers, why not make extra spiced chilli oil (opposite) from the Roast beef recipe on page 75 to accompany this dish?

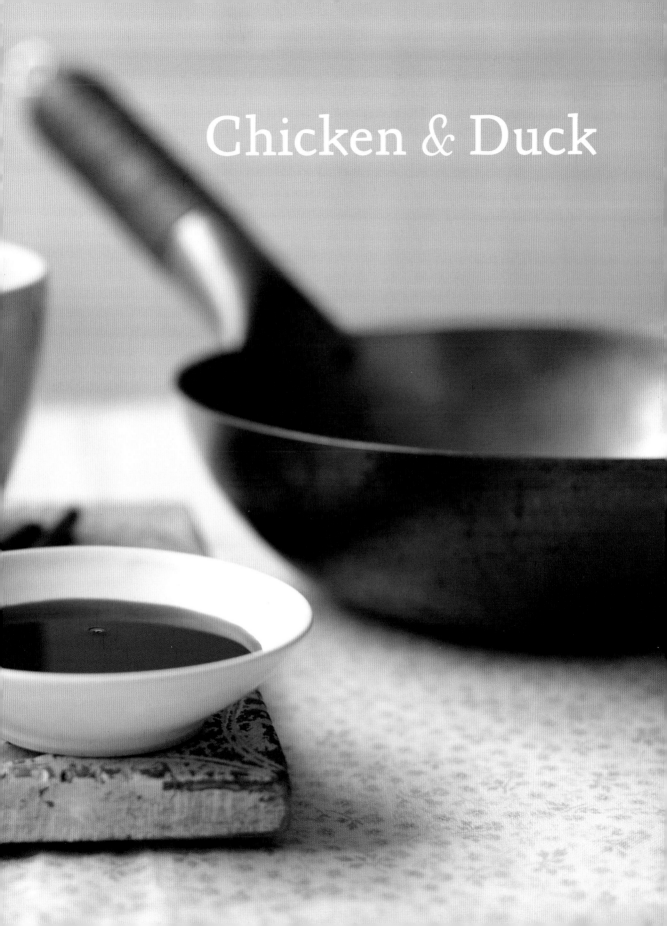

Chicken & Duck

Chicken & snake bean stir-fry	10 minutes (plus 20 minutes soaking/marinating)
Chicken & black bean stir-fry	15 minutes
Sweet & sour duck	15 minutes
Hot pink pepper/black pepper chicken	15 minutes
Steamed chicken with sour & spicy dressing and spinach	45–50 minutes
Fried sweet chilli chicken	15 minutes
Cold spicy chicken salad with hot dressing	10 minutes (plus 1 hour chilling)
Three-cup chicken	20 minutes
Chicken, smoky bacon & bamboo shoot stir-fry	15 minutes
Juicy chilli chicken & cashew nut	20 minutes
Curry chicken stir-fry	40 minutes

Chicken & snake bean stir-fry

This is a stir-fry inspired by a lunch I had with 'Ah-e' (Aunty) in Beijing. She cooked a simple but delicious chicken and snake bean stir-fry, and this is my quick version.

SERVES 2

250g/9oz skinless chicken breast, cut into strips

1 teaspoon Shaohsing rice wine or dry sherry

1 teaspoon dark soy sauce

cornflour

2 tablespoons groundnut oil

1 garlic clove, crushed and finely chopped

1 dried Chinese mushroom, pre-soaked in hot water for 20 minutes, then drained and sliced

100g/3½oz snake beans or trimmed French beans (see Ching's Tip)

50g/2oz toasted cashew nuts

25ml/1fl oz hot chicken stock

1 teaspoon light soy sauce

a dash of toasted sesame oil

1 pinch of ground white pepper

steamed jasmine rice to serve (see page 154)

1   Marinate the chicken in the rice wine or sherry and the dark soy sauce for 10–15 minutes.

2   Just before cooking, dust the chicken lightly with cornflour. Heat a wok over a high heat and add the groundnut oil. When the oil starts to smoke, add the garlic and mushroom and stir-fry for a few seconds, then add the chicken and stir-fry for a few minutes until slightly browned.

3   Add the beans and stir-fry for 2 minutes until tender, then add the cashew nuts.

4   Add the hot stock and season with the light soy sauce, sesame oil and white pepper. Serve immediately with jasmine rice.

Ching's Tip

- Snake beans can be found in the vegetable section of a good Chinese supermarket, or use some trimmed French beans as a substitute.

Prep time: 10 minutes,
cook in: 5 minutes

Chicken & black bean stir-fry

I adore fermented black beans and this is one of my favourite easy suppers. I add a touch of a good-quality yellow bean sauce for a savoury mellow edge to the dish.

SERVES 2 AS A MAIN OR 4 TO SHARE

1 tablespoon groundnut oil

5 garlic cloves, finely chopped

1 tablespoon freshly grated root ginger

1 medium red chilli, deseeded and chopped

1 bird's eye chilli, deseeded and chopped

1 tablespoon fermented salted black beans, washed and crushed

1 tablespoon yellow bean paste

450g/1lb skinless chicken breast, sliced

1 tablespoon Shaohsing rice wine or dry sherry

2 green peppers, deseeded and cut into chunks

200ml/7fl oz vegetable stock

1 tablespoon light soy sauce

1 tablespoon cornflour blended with 2 tablespoons cold water

steamed jasmine rice (see page 154) or egg-fried rice (see page 155) to serve

1 Heat a wok over a high heat and add the groundnut oil. When the oil starts to smoke, add the garlic, ginger and chillies and stir-fry for a few seconds. Then add the fermented black beans and yellow bean paste and stir quickly.

2 Add the chicken slices and stir-fry for 1 minute, keeping the ingredients moving in the wok. As the meat starts to turn opaque, add the rice wine or sherry.

3 Add the green peppers and stir-fry for 1 minute, then add the stock and bring to the boil. Season with the soy sauce, then add the blended cornflour and stir to thicken. Serve with jasmine rice or egg-fried rice.

Sweet & sour duck

The Cantonese are known for their love of sweet and sour combinations and this recipe comes from that region. It's a home-style dish – easy, fruity and ready in minutes. I hope you enjoy it.

SERVES 2 TO SHARE

2 x 250g/9oz duck breasts

1 teaspoon Shaohsing rice wine
   or dry sherry

2 tablespoons potato flour or
   cornflour

200ml/7fl oz groundnut oil

2.5cm/1 inch piece of fresh root
   ginger, peeled and finely sliced

1 red pepper, deseeded and cut
   into 1cm/½ inch chunks

juice of 2 small oranges

juice of 1 lime

1 tablespoon light soy sauce

sea salt and ground white pepper

a few fresh orange segments
   to garnish

egg-fried rice to serve
   (see page 155)

1 Remove the skin from the duck breasts and cut the duck into thin slices. Put the slices into a bowl with some salt, white pepper, the rice wine or sherry and the potato flour or cornflour and mix well.

2 Heat a wok over a high heat and add 200ml/7fl oz groundnut oil. Heat the oil to 180°C/350°F or until a cube of bread dropped in turns golden brown in 15 seconds and floats to the surface. Using a spider or slotted spoon, add the duck and shallow-fry for about 2 minutes until crispy on the outside.

3 Take the wok off the heat, remove the duck from the wok and drain on absorbent kitchen paper. Pour the oil from the wok through a sieve into a heatproof container and save to use later. Return 1 tablespoon oil to the wok and return the wok to a high heat. When the oil starts to smoke, add the ginger and stir-fry for a few seconds, then add the red pepper and stir-fry for 1 minute. Return the duck to the wok, season with the orange juice, lime juice and soy sauce and toss well.

4 Garnish with orange segments and serve immediately with egg-fried rice.

Hot pink pepper/black pepper chicken

If you have most of the ingredients in your storecupboard, all you'll have to do is pick up some chicken and you can have this on the table in no time.

SERVES 2

1 tablespoon groundnut oil

1 tablespoon freshly grated
  root ginger

2 long dried chillies

1 tablespoon pink peppercorns
  (see Ching's Tip)

2 chicken thighs, skin on, halved
  on the bone

2 chicken drumsticks, skin on,
  halved on the bone

1 tablespoon Shaohsing rice wine
  or dry sherry

1 tablespoon light soy sauce

1 pinch of salt

½ teaspoon ground dry-toasted
  Sichuan peppercorns (see
  page 39)

1 spring onion, chopped at an
  angle into chunky pieces about
  2.5cm/1 inch long (optional)

a dash of chilli oil (optional)

egg-fried rice to serve (see
  page 155)

1 Heat a wok over a high heat and add the groundnut
   oil. When the oil starts to smoke, add the ginger and
   dried chillies and stir-fry for a few seconds. Then
   add the pink peppercorns and stir well.

2 Add all the chicken and stir-fry until starting to
   brown, then add the rice wine or sherry and cook
   for 5–6 minutes, stirring constantly, until done.

3 Season with the soy sauce, salt and Sichuan
   peppercorns. Sprinkle with the spring onion and
   drizzle some chilli oil over, if you like, then serve
   immediately with egg-fried rice.

Ching's Tip

■ If you can't find pink peppercorns, use black
  peppercorns or even Sichuan peppercorns.

Fried sweet chilli chicken

This quick and easy fried chicken is delicious and addictive. You can use chicken breast but I love juicy chicken thighs on the bone. Serve with an icy cold beer and chips.

SERVES 2–4 TO SHARE

2 chicken thighs, skinned and halved on the bone

2 chicken drumsticks, skinned and halved on the bone

4 tablespoons cornflour

2 egg whites

groundnut oil for deep-frying

sea salt and ground white pepper

FOR THE SAUCE

3 garlic cloves, finely chopped

2.5cm/1 inch piece of fresh root ginger, peeled and sliced

1 medium red chilli, deseeded

6 tablespoons sweet chilli sauce

1 tablespoon light soy sauce

juice of 1 lime

1 small handful of freshly chopped coriander

1 Season the chicken pieces with salt and white pepper. Combine the cornflour and egg whites to make a batter.

2 Heat a wok over a high heat and fill it to one-third of its depth with groundnut oil. Heat the oil to 180°C/350°F or until a cube of bread dropped in turns golden brown in 15 seconds and floats to the surface.

3 Dip the chicken slices in the batter, then place in a spider, lower into the oil and deep-fry for about 5 minutes until crispy and golden. Lift out using the spider or tongs and drain on absorbent kitchen paper. Pour the oil from the wok through a sieve into a heatproof container.

4 To make the sauce, wipe out the wok and heat over a high heat. Add 1 tablespoon of the drained oil and, when it starts to smoke, add the garlic, ginger and chilli and stir-fry for a few seconds, then add the chilli sauce, soy sauce and lime juice. Mix well.

5 Return the chicken to the wok and turn to coat in the hot sauce, then stir in the coriander and serve immediately.

Cold spicy chicken salad with hot dressing

With its sweet spicy flavours, this makes a delightful refreshing summer salad. You can make it well in advance and leave to chill until you're ready to serve.

SERVES 2

300g/11oz steamed chicken breast, shredded

2 carrots, cut into julienne strips

1 cucumber, cut into julienne strips

1 spring onion, finely chopped

1 handful of finely chopped fresh coriander

100g/3½oz roasted salted cashew nuts to garnish

FOR THE DRESSING

1 teaspoon grated garlic (optional)

2 tablespoons light soy sauce

2 tablespoons Chinkiang black rice vinegar or balsamic vinegar

2 tablespoons toasted sesame oil

1 teaspoon chilli oil

1 teaspoon chilli sauce

½ teaspoon brown sugar

1 Place a layer of shredded chicken on a plate, then top with a layer each of carrot and cucumber and, finally, another layer of chicken. Sprinkle with the spring onion and chopped coriander and refrigerate for 1 hour.

2 Meanwhile, combine all the ingredients for the dressing in a bowl.

3 About 5 minutes before serving, pour the dressing over the salad, garnish with the cashew nuts and serve immediately.

Three-cup chicken

This Taiwanese recipe uses 1 cup of soy sauce, 1 cup of sesame oil and 1 cup of rice wine. You can vary the amounts but the final stir-fry should be slightly sticky.

SERVES 2–4 TO SHARE

1 tablespoon groundnut oil

5 garlic cloves, finely chopped

2.5cm/1 inch piece of fresh root ginger, peeled and sliced

500g/1lb 2oz chicken thighs and drumsticks, skinned and each piece halved on the bone

50ml/2fl oz light soy sauce

50ml/2fl oz toasted sesame oil

50ml/2fl oz Shaohsing rice wine or dry sherry

1 tablespoon brown sugar

1 small handful of Chinese basil leaves, or Thai or Italian sweet basil, plus extra to garnish

1 medium red chilli, deseeded and cut into strips (optional)

steamed jasmine rice to serve (see page 154)

1 Heat a wok over a high heat and add the groundnut oil. When the oil starts to smoke, add the garlic and ginger and stir-fry quickly for a few seconds. Then add the chicken and stir-fry for 2–3 minutes until it has browned. Add the soy sauce, sesame oil and rice wine or sherry and cook on a medium heat for 6 minutes. Stir well and add the sugar.

2 Bring to the boil, then turn the heat down and simmer for about 5 minutes until the sauce is reduced completely and the chicken is cooked. Turn off the heat. Stir in the basil leaves and leave to wilt slightly.

3 Pour onto a plate, garnish with chilli strips, if you like, and more basil leaves and serve immediately with jasmine rice.

Ching's Tip

■ Since you want a dry stir-fry here, it's important to use toasted sesame oil, which will reduce as it cooks, and not pure sesame oil, which will just keep on cooking and not reduce.

Chicken, smoky bacon & bamboo shoot stir-fry

This savoury stir-fry is quick and easy to make. It can also be adapted to a noodle dish — just add some cooked noodles at the end — making it an extremely versatile recipe.

SERVES 2 OR 4 TO SHARE

1 tablespoon groundnut oil

3 smoked bacon rashers, sliced

2 x 250g/9oz chicken breasts, each cut into 5mm/¼ inch slices

1 tablespoon Shaohsing rice wine or dry sherry

1 x 220g tin of bamboo shoots, drained

1 handful of bean sprouts

1–2 tablespoons light soy sauce

1 tablespoon oyster sauce

a dash of toasted sesame oil

1 spring onion, sliced

jasmine rice (see page 154), egg-fried rice (see page 155) or sweet potato jasmine rice (see page 137) to serve

1 Heat a wok over a high heat and add the groundnut oil. When the oil starts to smoke, add the bacon and stir-fry for 2 minutes until crispy. Add the chicken and stir-fry for 4 minutes. As the chicken turns from pink to opaque, add the rice wine or sherry. Add the bamboo shoots and bean sprouts and stir-fry for 1 minute, then season to taste with the soy sauce, oyster sauce and sesame oil.

2 Garnish with the spring onion and serve immediately with whichever rice you fancy.

Prep time: 10 minutes,
cook in: 10 minutes

Juicy chilli chicken & cashew nut

The traditional technique for making this dish involves three or four stages. However, I have adapted the recipe so that the chicken is cooked in no time, giving you a tasty meal in minutes.

SERVES 2

1 teaspoon potato flour or cornflour

1 tablespoon cold water

400g/14oz chicken thighs (3 thighs), skinned, de-boned and cut into 2cm/¾ inch chunks (see Ching's Tip)

½ teaspoon Chinese five-spice powder

2 tablespoons groundnut oil

1 teaspoon Sichuan peppercorns

1 teaspoon chilli bean paste

1 medium red chilli, deseeded and ground in a pestle and mortar

a dash of Shaohsing rice wine or dry sherry

100g/3½oz roasted salted cashew nuts

2 spring onions, sliced at an angle

1 teaspoon light soy sauce

½ lime

egg-fried rice (see page 155) or plain rice to serve

1 Combine the potato flour or cornflour with the cold water in a bowl and mix well. Add the chicken pieces and turn to coat, then season with five-spice powder.

2 Heat a wok over a high heat and add the groundnut oil. When the oil starts to smoke, add the Sichuan peppercorns, chilli bean paste and ground red chilli and stir-fry for 30 seconds. Add the chicken and leave to settle for 30 seconds, then add a dash of rice wine or sherry. Toss all the ingredients well and cook for 3–4 minutes until the chicken has turned virtually opaque.

3 Add the cashew nuts and cook for another minute, then add the spring onions, toss well and cook for another minute. Season to taste with soy sauce and add a squeeze of lime juice. Transfer to serving plates and serve with egg-fried rice or plain rice.

Ching's Tip

■ Chicken thigh meat is delicious and tender, and it's cheaper than breast too. To de-bone it, just use a small sharp knife and cut as close to the bone as possible, or get your butcher (or boyfriend) to do it for you.

Curry chicken stir-fry

I love this healthy delicious dish. Poaching the chicken with Chinese leaf, spring onions and star anise gives it more flavour and keeps the meat succulent. Make sure you keep the poaching liquid and serve it as a bowl of hot soup to moisten the rice.

SERVES 2

2 x 275g/10oz chicken breasts, skinned

1 tablespoon groundnut oil

1 medium red onion, sliced

1 red pepper, deseeded and sliced

2 spring onions, sliced at an angle into 4cm/1½ inch strips

1 handful of bean sprouts

1 tablespoon light soy sauce

sea salt and ground white pepper

plain rice to serve

FOR THE SPICE MARINADE

1 teaspoon ground turmeric

½ teaspoon chilli powder

½ teaspoon medium curry powder

½ teaspoon ground coriander

1 tablespoon chilli bean paste

1 tablespoon Shaohsing rice wine or dry sherry

FOR THE STOCK

100g/3½oz Chinese leaves, washed and shredded

2 star anise

2 spring onions, sliced lengthways into 5cm/2 inch strips

1 tablespoon Shaohsing rice wine, mijiu rice wine or dry sherry

2.5cm/1 inch piece of fresh root ginger, peeled and sliced

1 Combine all the ingredients for the spice marinade in a bowl and set aside.

2 Bring a pan of water to the boil, add all the ingredients for the stock and bring back to the boil. Turn the heat down to a simmer, add the chicken breasts and poach for 25 minutes. Remove any scum from the top of the stock while cooking. Season with salt and white pepper. Remove the cooked chicken breast and, when cool enough to handle, shred into bite-size chunks. Keep the stock on a very low heat. Toss the chicken in the spice marinade.

3 Heat a wok over a medium heat and add the groundnut oil. When the oil starts to smoke, add the red onion and stir-fry for 1–2 minutes. Add the spiced chicken and stir well, then add the red pepper, spring onions and bean sprouts and stir-fry for 1 minute. Season with the soy sauce.

4 Serve with plain rice and a small bowl of the hot chicken stock to ladle onto the rice to moisten it.

Ching's Tip

- To save time, you can poach the chicken in advance and reheat the stock when ready to serve.

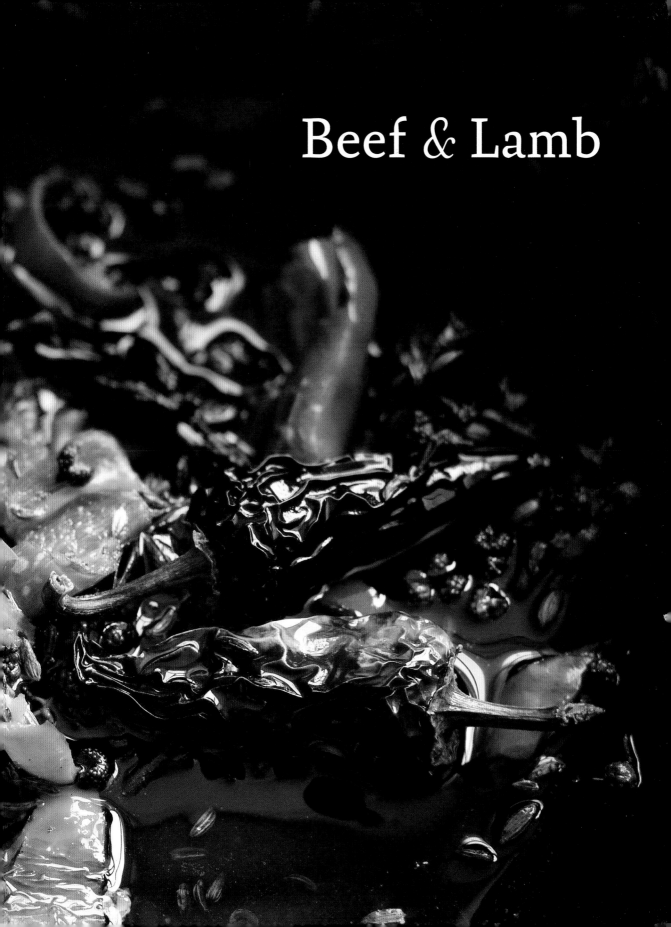

Beef & Lamb

Crispy Mongolian lamb	20 minutes (plus 20 minutes marinating)
Spicy chunky lamb	10 minutes (plus 10 minutes marinating)
Chongqing beef	15 minutes
Saucy beef dofu	15 minutes
Roast beef in 'four-spiced' chilli oil	7 minutes
Garlic chilli pepper beef & mushroom pak choy	10 minutes

Crispy Mongolian lamb

Using ready-made tortillas or fajitas makes this a quick and easy recipe. Or, for a healthier option, you could serve the lamb on lettuce leaves or a salad of cucumber, spring onion and sliced red and yellow peppers.

SERVES 2

250g/9oz lamb fillet, sliced

wheat flour tortillas or Mexican-style
    fajitas to serve (or make your own
    flatbreads, see opposite)

groundnut oil for shallow-frying

potato flour or cornflour

FOR THE MARINADE

1 tablespoon freshly grated root
    ginger

1 tablespoon Shaohsing rice wine or
    dry sherry

1 spring onion, finely chopped

1 teaspoon ground dry-toasted Sichuan
    peppercorns (see page 39)

½ teaspoon salt

1 teaspoon light soy sauce

1 teaspoon yellow bean sauce

1 teaspoon hoisin sauce

1 pinch of Chinese five-spice
    powder

TO SERVE

cucumber strips

spring onion slices

iceberg lettuce, torn into shreds

hoisin sauce

Ching's Tips

- If you're serving this with a salad instead of wraps, make a sweet honey, orange, hoisin sauce and olive oil dressing to complement the salad.
- You could also use pitta bread pockets – oiled, sprinkled with toasted sesame seeds and then grilled.

1 Put all the ingredients for the marinade into a bowl and stir to combine. Add the lamb and turn to coat, then cover the bowl and leave to marinate for 20 minutes, or overnight if possible, in the fridge. Preheat the oven to 140°C/275°F/gas mark 1, then put the tortillas or fajitas in to warm through.

2 Heat a wok over a high heat and fill to a quarter of its depth with groundnut oil. Heat the oil to 180°C/350°F or until a cube of bread dropped in turns golden brown in 15 seconds and floats to the surface. Lightly coat the lamb pieces in potato flour or cornflour, then, using a spider or slotted spoon, lower into the oil and fry until golden brown. Lift out using the spider or spoon and drain on absorbent kitchen paper.

3 To serve, place some crispy lamb in a tortilla, fajita (or sesame flatbread), add some cucumber strips, spring onion and lettuce, spoon over some hoisin sauce and eat.

Sesame flatbread

MAKES 8 SMALL
PIECES

125g/4oz plain flour, plus extra
  for dusting

2 pinches of salt

100ml/3½fl oz hot water

2 tablespoons groundnut oil

1–2 tablespoons toasted sesame
  oil

2–3 tablespoons white sesame
  seeds

1 Combine the flour and salt in a bowl, stir in the hot water and work into a dough. Turn out onto a floured surface and knead for 5 minutes until the dough is elastic and smooth. Oil the surface of the dough with a little of the groundnut oil. Place in a floured bowl, cover with a damp tea towel and leave to rest at room temperature for 20 minutes. Preheat the oven to 140°C/275°F/gas mark 1.

2 Roll out the dough into a long sausage shape and divide into four equal pieces. Using the palm of your hand, roll each piece into a ball and then flatten out with a rolling pin into a large disc. Brush with sesame oil and sprinkle some sesame seeds onto each disc. Reform into balls and roll into flat discs about 3mm/⅛ inch thick.

3 Heat the remaining groundnut oil in a large wok or pan, then add the flatbreads one at a time and toast them until golden brown. Lift out and place in a tray, cover with foil and keep warm in the oven until ready to serve.

Spicy chunky lamb

Fast, simple and healthy, this dish is inspired by the Muslim Chinese use of spices. First marinate the lamb in a delicious spice paste and then cook in the wok.

SERVES 2

300g/11oz lamb neck fillet, cut
   into 2cm/¾ inch cubes

1 tablespoon groundnut oil

1 medium onion, sliced

1 tablespoon Shaohsing rice wine
   or dry sherry

1 green pepper, deseeded and cut
   into chunks

sea salt and ground black pepper

steamed jasmine rice to serve
   (see page 154)

FOR THE SPICE PASTE

1 tablespoon groundnut oil

2 medium red chillies, deseeded
   and roughly chopped

1 teaspoon dried chilli flakes

1 teaspoon medium curry powder

1 teaspoon turmeric

1 teaspoon ground coriander

1 Put all the ingredients for the spice paste into a
   pestle and mortar and crush together well. Transfer
   to a bowl, add the lamb and turn to coat, then leave
   to marinate for 10 minutes.

2 Heat a wok over a high heat and add the groundnut
   oil. Add the onion and stir-fry for 1 minute, then push
   it to one side. Add the lamb and stir-fry for 1 minute,
   then, as the meat starts to turn brown, add the rice
   wine or sherry and cook for another minute. Add the
   green pepper and stir-fry for 1–2 minutes. Season
   with salt and black pepper and serve immediately
   with jasmine rice.

Roast beef in 'four-spiced' chilli oil

This is a quick and easy way to use up any leftover roast beef. The dressing is also great served over any roast meats or seafood. If you like chilli and spices, you won't be disappointed.

SERVES 2

350g/12oz cooked roast beef, sliced

1 tablespoon groundnut oil

4 dried red chillies

½ teaspoon cloves

½ teaspoon fennel seeds

2 star anise

1 tablespoon Sichuan peppercorns

2 medium green chillies, deseeded and bruised in a pestle and mortar

5 tablespoons chilli oil

1 tablespoon lemon juice

a few pinches of sea salt

1   Arrange the sliced beef on two serving plates.

2   Heat a wok over a high heat and add the groundnut oil. When the oil starts to smoke, add the dried chillies, cloves, fennel, star anise and Sichuan peppercorns and stir-fry for a few seconds. Add the green chillies and stir-fry for a few seconds, then add the chilli oil and lemon juice and season with salt.

3   Pour the hot oil over the beef slices and serve immediately.

Garlic chilli pepper beef & mushroom pak choy

Healthy, tasty and so fast, this recipe is one for your other half to make when you want to put your feet up and not have to wait an hour for dinner.

SERVES 2

2 x 275g/10oz sirloin beef steaks, each cut into 5mm/¼ inch slices

1 tablespoon groundnut oil

1 tablespoon Shaohsing rice wine or dry sherry

200g/7oz pak choy leaves, washed, stems and leaves separated and sliced

50g/2oz shiitake mushrooms, sliced

sea salt

steamed jasmine rice (see page 154), green salad or spicy wild rice salad (see page 146) to serve

FOR THE MARINADE

6 garlic cloves, crushed

2 medium green chillies, deseeded and finely chopped

1 tablespoon chilli paste

1 tablespoon light soy sauce

½ teaspoon brown sugar

ground black pepper

1 Put all the ingredients for the marinade into a bowl and stir to combine. Trim the fat off the beef, add the meat to the marinade and toss for a few minutes.

2 Heat a wok over a high heat and add the groundnut oil. When the oil starts to smoke, add the beef (reserve the marinade) and cook for 1 minute, then add the rice wine or sherry. Add the pak choy stems and cook for 1 minute, then add the leaves and mushrooms and cook for another minute. Add the reserved marinade and cook for another minute. Season further to taste with salt and serve immediately with jasmine rice, salad or my spicy wild rice salad.

Fish

Steamed wine sea bass	20 minutes (plus 20 minutes soaking)
Dofu ru haddock	11 minutes
Chilli bean cod	11 minutes
Sweet & sour monkfish fillets	18 minutes
Spicy bacon crispy haddock	13 minutes
Ginger, chilli & soy-steamed cod	13 minutes
Breaded haddock with Sichuan pepper, chilli & salt	25 minutes
Sweet & smoky 'hong sao yu'	15 minutes

Steamed wine sea bass

This dish is healthy, quick and easy. The large quantity of rice wine used provides a fragrant bittersweet flavour and works wonderfully well with all the ingredients.

SERVES 2 TO SHARE

1 whole fresh sea bass (about 350g/12oz), head on, or other white-fleshed fish

5cm/2 inch piece of fresh root ginger, peeled and sliced

100g/3½oz roast ham, sliced (optional)

4 dried Chinese mushrooms, pre-soaked in hot water for 20 minutes, then drained, stalks removed and sliced, or 4 fresh shiitake mushrooms, sliced

4 tablespoons Shaohsing rice wine or dry sherry

salt and ground white pepper

2 spring onions, sliced lengthways into 7.5cm/3 inch strips, to garnish

steamed jasmine rice (see page 154) and stir-fried vegetables to serve

1 Rinse the fish in cold running water and pat dry with absorbent kitchen paper, then place on a heatproof plate. Cut some slits into the skin on both sides and season with salt and white pepper. Stuff the ginger, ham, if using, and mushrooms into the slits and inside the fish and season with rice wine or sherry. Place the plate in a bamboo steamer and cover with the lid.

2 Heat a wok over a high heat and fill to three-quarters of its depth with water, then bring to the boil. Place the steamer on top (making sure the water does not touch the base of the steamer) and steam for 8–9 minutes until the fish is cooked and the flesh flakes when poked with a knife.

3 Lay the spring onions on top of the fish, remove the steamer and keep the lid closed until ready to serve. Serve with jasmine rice and stir-fried vegetables.

Ching's Tip

- You can use any white-fleshed fish for this dish.

Dofu ru haddock

Another simple, quick and tasty fish dish. Dofu ru is a fermented bean curd used in marinades. It is extremely salty in flavour so you need only one cube per fillet.

SERVES 2

2 x 200g/7oz haddock fillets

2 cubes of brown dofu ru
(fermented bean curd, see
Ching's Tip) or 2 tablespoons
miso paste

2 garlic cloves, grated

2 teaspoons freshly grated root
ginger

1 tablespoon honey

2 tablespoons groundnut oil

1 tablespoon Shaohsing rice wine
or dry sherry

1 tablespoon light soy sauce

sea salt

1 spring onion, finely sliced,
to garnish

citrusy salad to serve
(see page 131)

1 Rinse the fish in cold running water and pat dry with absorbent kitchen paper. Place the fish in a shallow bowl and rub the flesh well with the dofu ru cubes or miso paste. Add the garlic, ginger and honey and massage well into the fish.

2 Heat a griddle pan on a high heat and add the groundnut oil. When the oil starts to smoke, place the fish on the griddle, skin side down. Using your fingers, press down onto the fish for 30 seconds to prevent it from curling upwards, then cook for 2 minutes. As the flesh turns from translucent to opaque, pour the rice wine or sherry over the fillets. Cook for a further 3–4 minutes until the flesh of the fish has turned opaque and is quite firm to the touch.

3 Season with the soy sauce and salt to taste. Garnish with spring onion and serve with my citrusy salad.

Ching's Tip

- Dofu ru is available in white, brown and red varieties, depending on what spices have been used to flavour it. The brown variety uses a combination of spices, soy sauce and fermented soya beans.

Chilli bean cod

This is a very tasty supper that can be made in minutes and is great served with the stir-fry. Do buy cod from a sustainable source.

SERVES 2

2 x 225g/8oz cod fillets, skin on

2 tablespoons chilli bean paste

2 teaspoons freshly grated root ginger

2 tablespoons groundnut oil

1 tablespoon Shaohsing rice wine or dry sherry

1 tablespoon light soy sauce

sea salt and ground white pepper

a few sprigs of fresh coriander, finely chopped, to garnish

2 lemon wedges (optional)

Garlic pak choy exotic mushroom stir-fry (see page 127) and jasmine rice (see page 154) to serve

1 Rinse the fish in cold running water and pat dry with absorbent kitchen paper. Place the fish in a shallow bowl, add the chilli bean paste and rub well into the flesh of the fish, then add the ginger and massage in well.

2 Heat a griddle pan on a high heat and add the groundnut oil. When the oil starts to smoke, place the fish on the griddle, skin side down. Using your fingers, press down onto the fish for 30 seconds to prevent it from curling upwards, then cook for 2 minutes. As the flesh turns from translucent to opaque, pour the rice wine or sherry over the fillets. Cook for a further 3–4 minutes until the flesh of the fish has turned opaque and is quite firm to the touch.

3 Season with the soy sauce and salt and pepper to taste. Garnish with chopped coriander and serve with a wedge of lemon, jasmine rice and the stir-fry.

Sweet & sour monkfish fillets

This is my quick and easy version of a carp dish I ate in Hangzhou, in northwest China. Here I'm using monkfish fillet, which is meaty and won't break apart when cooked in this way.

SERVES 2

350g/12oz monkfish fillet, skinned

steamed jasmine rice to serve (see page 154)

FOR THE SAUCE

1 tablespoon groundnut oil

2 garlic cloves, crushed and finely chopped

1 tablespoon freshly grated root ginger

1 red pepper, deseeded and cut into 1.5 x 1.5cm/⅝ x ⅝ inch chunks

75g/3oz pineapple chunks, fresh or tinned, diced

2 tablespoons clear rice vinegar or cider vinegar

2 tablespoons light soy sauce

100ml/3½fl oz pineapple juice

1 teaspoon brown sugar

1 tablespoon cornflour blended with 2 tablespoons cold water

FOR THE GARNISH

1 spring onion, sliced

1 small handful of fresh coriander, roughly chopped

1 Rinse the fish in cold running water and pat dry with absorbent kitchen paper, then cut into 5cm/2 inch chunks and place in a spider. Heat a pan of water until boiling, then lower the spider into the pan and poach the fillets for about 3 minutes until the flesh has turned opaque and flakes when poked with a knife. Lift out, transfer to a serving plate and keep to one side.

2 Heat a small wok over a high heat and add the groundnut oil. When the oil starts to smoke, add the garlic and ginger and stir-fry for a few seconds, then add the red pepper and pineapple and stir-fry until tender. Add the vinegar, soy sauce, pineapple juice and sugar and bring to the boil, then stir in the blended cornflour to thicken the sauce.

3 Place the fish fillets on a plate, pour the sauce over them and garnish with the spring onion and coriander. Serve with jasmine rice.

Ching's Tip

■ To give the sauce a reddy colour, you can cheat and add a tablespoon of ketchup.

Sweet & smoky 'hong sao yu'

'Hong sao yu' in Mandarin means 'red-cooked fish' — 'hong sao' describes the deep brown colour that comes from combining soy sugar and spices. Ready in minutes, this is an elegant dish for entertaining.

SERVES 2

350g/12oz cod fillet, skin on

1 tablespoon Shaohsing rice wine
   or dry sherry

2 tablespoons groundnut oil

1–2 tablespoons potato flour
   or cornflour

sea salt

Mum's sweet potato jasmine rice
   to serve (see page 137)

FOR THE SAUCE

200ml/7fl oz water

2.5cm/1 inch piece of fresh root
   ginger, peeled and finely sliced

1 star anise

1 cinnamon stick

1 teaspoon Sichuan peppercorns

1 tablespoon light soy sauce

1 teaspoon dark soy sauce

1 tablespoon Chinkiang black rice
   vinegar or balsamic vinegar

2 tablespoons brown sugar

1 Rinse the fish in cold running water and pat dry with absorbent kitchen paper, then cut into 5cm/2 inch chunks. Place in a bowl with the rice wine or sherry and leave to marinate for a few minutes, then pat dry.

2 Heat a wok over a high heat and add the groundnut oil. When the oil starts to smoke, dip the fish slices in the potato flour or cornflour and fry on a medium heat until crisp and the flesh has turned opaque and flakes when poked with a knife. Leave the fish in the wok and turn the heat down to very low.

3 Heat another small wok over a medium heat, add all the ingredients for the sauce and cook for about 4 minutes to reduce the sauce by half. Sieve the sauce over the fish in the other wok (retaining the sieved spices), then turn the heat up to medium and cook until the sauce bubbles. Spoon the sauce over the fish, coating it well.

4 To serve, transfer the cod into a bowl and pour the sauce over it, then sprinkle the spices sieved from the wok over the top. Serve immediately with sweet potato jasmine rice.

Ching's Tip

■ You could also cook beef, pork or chicken slices in the same way.

Shellfish

Razor clams with lardons & bamboo shoots	20 minutes
Exploding river prawns	20 minutes
Black bean razor clams	18 minutes
Wok-fried octopus with garlic coriander salsa	13 minutes
Rice wine tomato king prawns	18 minutes
Squid & crevettes in chilli tomato sauce	13 minutes
Sichuan-style sweet & sour prawns	18 minutes
Prawn & chilli bamboo shoot stir-fry	18 minutes
Taiwan-inspired 'teriyaki' squid	20 minutes (plus 20 minutes marinating/soaking)

Razor clams with lardons & bamboo shoots

In Fujian, ingredients are cooked simply to bring out their natural flavours. In the spirit of their cuisine, I have fused two tasty ingredients – sweet fresh razor clams and crunchy bamboo shoots. Easy and delicious.

SERVES 2

200g/7oz razor clams in shell, washed (see Ching's Tip)

1 tablespoon groundnut oil

2 tablespoons freshly grated root ginger

100g/3½oz lardons, or smoky bacon, cut into 1cm/½ inch thick chunks

2 tablespoons Shaohsing rice wine or dry sherry

200ml/7fl oz hot vegetable stock

1 x 220g tin of bamboo shoots, drained and sliced

1 tablespoon light soy sauce

1 pinch of ground white pepper

1 tablespoon cornflour blended with 2 tablespoons cold water

a dash of toasted sesame oil

1 large handful of finely chopped fresh coriander

steamed jasmine rice to serve (see page 154)

1 The razor clam shells should close when tapped, so discard any open shells. Heat a wok over a high heat and add the groundnut oil. When the oil starts to smoke, add the ginger first and then the lardons and stir-fry quickly for a few seconds until fragrant. Add the razor clams and stir-fry for 2 minutes (which may need a bit of manoeuvring because the clams are long), then add the rice wine or sherry and the hot stock and cook for 3–4 minutes until the clams open. Add the bamboo shoots. Discard any clams that haven't opened.

2 Season with the soy sauce and white pepper, then bring to the boil, add the blended cornflour and stir to thicken. Add a dash of sesame oil, stir in the coriander and serve immediately with jasmine rice.

Ching's Tip

■ When you buy fresh razor clams from the fishmonger, pack them in ice to keep them fresh, or keep them wrapped in paper in the fridge and use them within 24 hours. Before cooking, just wash the clams in cold water and scrub off any dirt on the shells.

Exploding river prawns

I had these delightfully crunchy prawns in Shanghai this summer. They were so good you could eat the whole prawn if you dared – I removed the head but I did eat the rest, including the shell.

SERVES 2

groundnut oil for shallow-frying

300g/11oz small raw sea prawns, shell, tail and heads on

cornflour

2 garlic cloves, finely chopped

1 tablespoon freshly grated root ginger

1 medium red chilli, deseeded and finely chopped

1 tablespoon Shaohsing rice wine or dry sherry

2 tablespoons Longjing tea leaves

1 tablespoon light soy sauce

1 pinch of salt

1 pinch of sugar

coriander sprigs to garnish

mixed salad to serve

FOR THE CRISPY GARNISH

2 tablespoons finely chopped garlic cloves

2 tablespoons finely chopped shallots

2 tablespoons Longjing tea leaves

cornflour

1 pinch of salt

1 pinch of sugar

Wok-fried octopus with garlic coriander salsa

Inspired by Hong Kong's wonderful seafood, I decided to make a simple dish of pan-fried octopus served with a garlic, coriander and lemon dipping sauce. Fast and easy!

SERVES 2

1 tablespoon groundnut oil

2 shallots, finely chopped

250g/9oz octopus tentacles, washed and cut into similar-size pieces

freshly chopped coriander to garnish

lemon wedges to serve (optional)

FOR THE SALSA VERDE

2 garlic cloves

1 small handful of fresh coriander

2 lemon slices

1 teaspoon lemon juice

1 red chilli, deseeded and sliced

2 tablespoons light soy sauce

1 tablespoon groundnut oil

sea salt

1 Heat a wok over a high heat and add the groundnut oil. When the oil starts to smoke, add the shallots and stir-fry until translucent. Next, add the octopus tentacles and stir-fry until tender and the octopus has turned a more opaque pink than a translucent purple. Once cooked, transfer to a shallow serving bowl.

2 Pound all the ingredients for the salsa verde in a pestle and mortar to make a rough and ready paste, then pour into a shallow dressing bowl.

3 Garnish the octopus with coriander and serve with lemon wedges and the salsa verde.

Ching's Tip

- If you are not a fan of octopus, try a medley of prawns, squid rings and mussels.

Rice wine tomato king prawns

If you like cooked tomatoes and shellfish then this is the perfect dish for you. It's an easy healthy supper that takes minutes to make. The results are fresh, juicy, tangy and delicious.

SERVES 2 AS A MAIN OR 4 TO SHARE

1 tablespoon groundnut oil

2 garlic cloves, finely chopped

1 tablespoon freshly grated root ginger

2 ripe red tomatoes, sliced into wedges, tops discarded

10 large raw tiger prawns, shelled with head off, tail on, and deveined

3 tablespoons mijiu rice wine, mirin, vodka or sake

1 small handful of fresh coriander, finely chopped

sea salt and ground black pepper

steamed jasmine rice to serve (see page 154)

1 Heat a wok over a high heat and add the groundnut oil. When the oil starts to smoke, add the garlic and ginger and stir-fry for a few seconds. Add the tomatoes and stir-fry for 30 seconds, then add the tiger prawns. As the prawns start to turn pink, add the rice wine or vodka and cook until the prawns have all turned pink. Season with salt and black pepper, then toss in the chopped coriander and mix well. Transfer to a serving plate and serve immediately with jasmine rice.

Ching's Tip

■ Ripe juicy red tomatoes and fresh large tiger prawns are a must for this dish.

Prep time: 10 minutes,
cook in: 3 minutes

Squid & crevettes in chilli tomato sauce

This is really easy and takes just minutes to cook – a tasty more-ish dish.

SERVES 2

1 tablespoon groundnut oil

1 medium green chilli, deseeded and finely chopped

200g/7oz squid rings

9 (about 160g/5½oz) large crevettes (Mediterranean prawns)

1 tablespoon Shaohsing rice wine or dry sherry

1 tablespoon light soy sauce

1 small handful of freshly chopped coriander

steamed jasmine rice (see page 154) and stir-fried vegetables, to serve

FOR THE CHILLI TOMATO SAUCE

1 medium onion, diced

1 medium red chilli, deseeded and roughly chopped

2 small ripe red tomatoes, roughly chopped

2 tablespoons tomato ketchup

1 tablespoon soft brown sugar

1 tablespoon light soy sauce

1 Put all the ingredients for the chilli tomato sauce into a blender and whiz to a paste.

2 Heat a wok over a high heat and add the groundnut oil. When the oil starts to smoke, add the green chilli and stir-fry for a few seconds. Add the squid and crevettes and cook for 30 seconds, then add the rice wine or sherry. Add the chilli tomato sauce and bring to the bubble, then season further to taste with the soy sauce.

3 Add the chopped coriander and stir through, then serve immediately with jasmine rice and stir-fried vegetables.

Sichuan-style sweet & sour prawns

Ketchup may not be a gourmet ingredient but it contains lycopene, which is good for you, and here it provides a delicious sweetness and great colour, while the Sichuan peppercorns provide the numbing spicy heat.

SERVES 2 AS A MAIN OR 4 TO SHARE

1 egg

100g/3½oz potato flour or
  cornflour

2 tablespoons water

600ml/1 pint groundnut oil,
  plus 1 tablespoon

12 large raw tiger prawns, head and
  shell off, tail on, and deveined

1 tablespoon Sichuan peppercorns

5 garlic cloves, finely chopped

2.5cm/1 inch piece of fresh root
  ginger, peeled and grated

2 medium red chillies, deseeded
  and finely chopped

1 tablespoon lime juice

2 spring onions, chopped at an angle
  into 2.5cm/1 inch long pieces

1 small handful of fresh coriander,
  finely chopped

steamed jasmine rice (see page 154)
  and deep-fried vegetables
  (optional, see Ching's Tip)
  to serve

FOR THE SAUCE

200ml/7fl oz hot water

5 tablespoons tomato ketchup

1 tablespoon soft brown sugar

1 tablespoon light soy sauce

2 teaspoons cornflour

Prep time: 15 minutes, cook in: 5 minutes
(plus 20 minutes marinating/soaking)

Taiwan-inspired 'teriyaki' squid

On a recent visit to Taiwan I had this as a street snack — a large butterflied cuttlefish, marinated in a garlicky, sweet soy dressing and then barbequed with chilli paste. This is my quick and easy version.

SERVES 2

6 whole baby squid (10cm/4 inch long), cleaned

3 garlic cloves, finely chopped

3 tablespoons light soy sauce

3 tablespoons mijiu rice wine, mirin, vodka or sake

3 tablespoons soft brown sugar

TO SERVE

ground chilli powder, cayenne pepper or smoked paprika

white sesame seeds, toasted until brown

citrusy salad (see page 131)

1 Cut the head and tentacles off the body of the squid. Slice off the tentacles and put to one side. Discard the head. Slice through one side of the body of each squid from top to bottom and open out. Put the garlic, soy sauce, rice wine or vodka and the sugar into a bowl. Add the squid and turn to coat, then leave to marinate for 20 minutes. Meanwhile, soak six bamboo skewers in cold water for 20 minutes.

2 Skewer each squid right through from base to top, then place the tentacles on the top of each skewer. Retain the marinade.

3 Heat a griddle pan on a high heat. Place the squid on the griddle and cook for 1 minute on one side. Brush with the reserved marinade, flip the squid over and cook for another minute, brushing with the reserved marinade to baste. Cook until the squid has turned opaque, the flesh is slightly firm to the touch and the marinade coating on the squid has turned sticky.

4 Dust with chilli powder, cayenne pepper or smoked paprika and sprinkle with sesame seeds, then serve immediately with the citrusy salad.

Vegetarian & Side Dishes

Sweetcorn, egg & spring onion stir-fry	10 minutes
Spicy Sichuan aubergine	22 minutes
Oriental mushrooms & dofu in garlic black bean sauce	16 minutes
Garlic spinach	7 minutes
Egg & tomato spring onion stir-fry	10 minutes
Lotus root crisps	35 minutes (plus 10 minutes soaking)
Spicy red cabbage	15 minutes (plus 30 minutes resting and chilling)
Garlic pak choy exotic mushroom stir-fry	10 minutes
Spicy red cabbage & edamame beans	7 minutes (plus 20 minutes chilling)
Citrusy salad	10 minutes

Sweetcorn, egg & spring onion stir-fry

This is a popular side dish and makes a great accompaniment to salty food. It's also a good dish to serve to children, as they love the sweetness and crunchy texture of the sweetcorn.

SERVES 4 TO SHARE

3 eggs, beaten

1 teaspoon cornflour blended with 1 tablespoon cold water

1 tablespoon groundnut oil

1 x 200g tin of sweetcorn, drained

1 large spring onion, finely chopped

1 tablespoon light soy sauce

sea salt and ground white pepper

a dash of toasted sesame oil

1 Beat the eggs in a bowl, then stir in the blended cornflour.

2 Heat a wok over a high heat and add the groundnut oil. When the oil starts to smoke, add the sweetcorn and stir-fry for a few seconds. Pour in the beaten eggs and leave to settle for 1–2 minutes, then swirl the liquid egg around the wok and, using a wooden spoon, stir to scramble it. Add the spring onion – the spring onion and sweetcorn should stick to the egg with the help of the cornflour paste. Season with the soy sauce, salt, white pepper and a dash of sesame oil and serve immediately.

Ching's Tip

■ You can use fresh corn or tinned, it's up to you.

Spicy Sichuan aubergine

This spicy dish, also known as Yu Shiang Cie Tze, is bursting with heat and flavour and has a delicate savoury tang from the black rice vinegar. This is definitely a winter favourite.

SERVES 2–4 TO SHARE

groundnut oil for deep-frying

1 large aubergine, sliced lengthways into 2cm/¾ inch wide x 4cm/1½ inch long, chunky batons

2 garlic cloves, finely chopped

2.5cm/1 inch piece of fresh root ginger, peeled and finely chopped

1 medium red chilli, with seeds, sliced into rings

2 tablespoons chilli bean paste

200ml/7fl oz hot vegetable stock

1 tablespoon light soy sauce

1 tablespoon Chinkiang black rice vinegar or balsamic vinegar

2 pinches of brown sugar

1 tablespoon cornflour blended with 2 tablespoons cold water

1 spring onion, finely chopped

egg-fried rice to serve (see page 155)

1 Heat a wok over a high heat, then fill the wok to one-third of its depth with groundnut oil. Heat the oil to 180°C/350°F or until a cube of bread dropped in turns golden brown in 15 seconds and floats to the surface.

2 Pat the aubergine dry and, using tongs, lower each piece into the oil and deep-fry for 3 minutes until slightly golden, the skin slightly wrinkled and the flesh soft but still retaining its shape. Remove from the oil and drain on absorbent kitchen paper.

3 Pour the oil from the wok through a sieve into a heatproof container (you can use it to make delicious stir-fries). Return 1 tablespoon oil to the wok and heat until smoking, then add the garlic, ginger and sliced chilli and stir-fry quickly for a few seconds. Stir in the chilli bean paste and return the aubergines to the wok. Add the hot stock and bring to the boil, then turn the heat down to medium and simmer for 3 minutes until all the aubergine is soft and creamy.

4 Season with the soy sauce, vinegar and sugar, then add the blended cornflour and stir to thicken the sauce. Sprinkle with the spring onion for a fresh bite and serve immediately with egg-fried rice.

119

Oriental mushrooms & dofu in garlic black bean sauce

The dofu soaks up the sauce like a sponge and provides texture, the chilli gives a delightful mild kick and the earthy mushrooms give the sauce added flavour.

SERVES 4

1 tablespoon vegetable oil

60g/2½oz oyster mushrooms, sliced

100g/3½oz fresh shiitake
  mushrooms, sliced

100g/3½oz fried dofu (bean curd),
  cut into 2cm/¾ inch squares

200ml/7fl oz hot chicken stock

1 tablespoon light soy sauce

1½ tablespoons cornflour blended
  with 3 tablespoons cold water
  (optional)

fresh enoki mushrooms to garnish

FOR THE BLACK BEAN SAUCE

1 tablespoon fermented salted
  black beans, washed

1 tablespoon light soy sauce

2 garlic cloves, crushed

1 red chilli, deseeded and chopped

1 tablespoon Shaohsing rice wine
  or dry sherry

1 Put all the ingredients for the black bean sauce into a food processor and blitz briefly – do not process to a smooth sauce, you want to keep some texture.

2 Heat a wok over a high heat and add the vegetable oil. When the oil starts to smoke, throw in the oyster and shiitake mushrooms and the dofu and stir-fry for less than 1 minute.

3 Add the sauce and stir gently, taking care not to break the dofu.

4 Add the hot stock to the wok and bring to the boil, then season with the soy sauce. For a thicker sauce, add the blended cornflour and stir well.

5 Serve garnished with some enoki mushrooms.

Ching's Tip

- This is great with roasted chicken or turkey slices and garlic baby pak choy.

Prep time: 5 minutes, cook in: 30 minutes
(plus 10 minutes soaking)

Lotus root crisps

These salt- and vinegar-flavoured lotus root crisps are really crunchy and take no time to prepare.

SERVES 4

500ml/18fl oz cold water

4 tablespoons clear rice vinegar or cider vinegar

3 lotus root sections, topped and tailed, then peeled and sliced using a mandolin

groundnut oil for deep-frying

sea salt and ground black pepper

1 Preheat the oven to 110°C/225°F/Gas ¼. Put the water and vinegar into a bowl and mix well. Add the lotus root slices and soak for 10 minutes. Drain well, then dry on absorbent kitchen paper.

2 Heat a wok or pan over a high heat, then fill the wok to one-third of its depth with groundnut oil. Heat the oil to 180°C/350°F or until a cube of bread dropped in turns golden brown in 15 seconds and floats to the surface. Using a slotted spoon, lower about one-fifth of the lotus root into the oil and deep-fry for about 6 minutes until golden. Remove and drain on absorbent kitchen paper, then cover with foil and put in the oven. Cook and drain the remainder in four more batches in the same way.

3 Transfer the lotus root to a bowl, season with salt and black pepper and toss well, then serve immediately.

Ching's Tip

■ Lotus roots were thought to originate from northeastern China 1,300 years ago. They are the long, hardy, connected 'stems' of the lotus flower and have a distinctive shape when sliced – like the head of a watering can. Similar in flavour to a water chestnut (and called 'Lian-ou' in Mandarin), they can be pickled and eaten in salads, or cooked in braised dishes and stir-fries, or deep-fried. They can be eaten raw but it's always best to blanch them in case of any bacteria. I always peel them too.

Prep time: 5 minutes, cook in: 2 minutes
(plus 20 minutes chilling)

Spicy red cabbage & edamame beans

I love making this chilled salad using the spicy cabbage on page 126. Forget peanuts, this makes a great tangy and fiery starter to get the taste buds going.

SERVES 4

100g/3½oz spicy red cabbage
   (see page 126)

100g/3½oz frozen podded
   edamame beans, boiled for
   2 minutes and drained

1 tablespoon light soy sauce

1 tablespoon toasted sesame oil

1 teaspoon rice vinegar

1 Toss all the ingredients together in a bowl and chill for 20 minutes.

2 Serve in small Chinese tea cups with chopsticks.

Ching's Tip

■ Edamame beans, otherwise known as fresh soya beans, can be found in the frozen food aisles of most supermarkets. They are firm and have great texture.

Citrusy salad

This citrusy salad is fruity and refreshing and will make a great accompaniment to any meal if you are not in the mood for rice. Make ahead of time and chill until needed.

SERVES 4

150g/5oz mixed salad leaves

12 ripe green seedless grapes, sliced in half

12 pink grapefruit segments

1 yellow pepper, deseeded and sliced

1 red pepper, deseeded and sliced

mustard cress leaves

FOR THE DRESSING

2 tablespoons groundnut oil

1 tablespoon light soy sauce

1 tablespoon lemon juice

3 tablespoons orange juice

1 pinch of ground white pepper

1 Put all the ingredients for the dressing into a bowl and mix well.

2 Divide all the salad ingredients equally between four serving bowls. Cover and chill in the fridge until ready to serve.

3 Just before serving, drizzle the dressing over each bowl and serve immediately.

Noodles & Rice

Shanghai-style crabmeat & egg noodle	15 minutes
Mum's sweet potato jasmine rice	40 minutes
Mixed seafood crispy noodle	30 minutes
Chicken rice	40 minutes (plus 20 minutes soaking)
Spicy Sichuan pepper prawn-fried rice	30 minutes
Taiwanese ginger & sesame chicken noodle soup	30 minutes
Spicy wild rice salad	15 minutes (plus 20 minutes chilling)
Rice wine pepper beef noodles	18 minutes (plus 10–20 minutes marinating)
Cantonese-style duck with rice	30 minutes (plus 20 minutes marinating, and 12 minutes resting)
Spicy fragrant minced pork with pickled soy 'lettuce', spinach rice	15 minutes
Jasmine rice	20–25 minutes
Egg-fried rice	15 minutes

Mixed seafood crispy noodle

Although there are a lot of ingredients in this recipe, it takes no time to cook.

SERVES 2

FOR THE CRISPY NOODLE

250g/9oz dried yellow shi wheat flour noodles or egg noodles

groundnut oil

FOR THE SAUCY SEAFOOD STIR-FRY

1 tablespoon groundnut oil

5 garlic cloves, finely chopped

1 tablespoon freshly grated root ginger

200g/7oz raw tiger prawns, shelled and deveined

1 tablespoon Shaohsing rice wine or dry sherry

75g/3oz fried fish cakes

75g/3oz fried fish balls

75g/3oz oyster mushrooms

75g/3oz broccoli, chopped into bite-size pieces

50g/2oz carrots, sliced

100g/3½oz Chinese cabbage, washed and cut into 2cm/¾ inch slices

250ml/9fl oz hot vegetable stock

1 handful of bean sprouts

2 tablespoons light soy sauce

2 tablespoons oyster sauce

1 tablespoon clear rice vinegar or cider vinegar

2 tablespoons cornflour blended with 2 tablespoons cold water

1 tablespoon toasted sesame oil

2 spring onions, finely sliced

1 small handful of fresh coriander, roughly chopped

1 Cook the noodles according to the packet instructions. Drain well, drizzle with some groundnut oil to keep them from sticking together and then set aside.

2 Fill a shallow pan with groundnut oil to a depth of 2cm/¾ inch. Heat the oil to 180°C/350°F or until a cube of bread dropped in turns golden brown in 15 seconds.

3 Add half the noodles to the oil and shallow-fry until golden and crispy. Drain on absorbent kitchen paper. Add the remaining noodles and repeat.

4 Next, make the stir-fry. Heat a wok over a high heat and add 1 tablespoon groundnut oil. When the oil starts to smoke, add the garlic and ginger and stir-fry for a few seconds, then add the prawns and, as they start to turn pink, add the rice wine or sherry. Add the fish cakes and fish balls and cook for less than 1 minute.

5 Add the mushrooms, broccoli, carrots and Chinese cabbage and stir-fry for 1 minute, then add the hot stock, bean sprouts, soy sauce, oyster sauce and vinegar and bring to the boil. Add the blended cornflour and stir to thicken. Season with the sesame oil, then add the spring onions and coriander.

6 To serve, place a batch of crispy noodles on each plate, ladle a portion of stir-fry on top and serve immediately.

Ching's Tip

■ If you fancy a healthier version, just boil the noodles as usual and, instead of deep-frying them, add them to the dish at the end of the cooking process and mix in.

Prep time: 10 minutes, cook in: 30 minutes
(plus 20 minutes soaking)

Chicken rice

Chicken rice or 'Bi-ge' is a traditional Taiwanese dish served on the day of the 'winter festival', where the chicken and rice are steamed together and served in bamboo baskets. This is my home-style version – easy to make and delicious.

SERVES 4–6 TO SHARE

1 tablespoon groundnut oil

5cm/2 inch piece of fresh root ginger, peeled and sliced

6 dried Chinese mushrooms, pre-soaked in hot water for 20 minutes, then drained and sliced, stalks removed

400g/14oz chicken thighs, skinned and halved on the bone (see Ching's Tips)

100ml/3½fl oz Shaohsing rice wine or dry sherry

100ml/3½fl oz pure sesame oil (see Ching's Tips)

½ teaspoon salt

300g/11oz jasmine rice

500ml/18fl oz water

garlic spinach to serve (see page 122)

1 Heat a wok over a high heat and add the groundnut oil. When the oil starts to smoke, add the ginger and stir-fry for 1 minute, then add the mushrooms and cook for 30 seconds. Add the chicken and stir-fry until starting to turn opaque, then add the rice wine or sherry and the sesame oil and cook for 2 minutes. Season with the salt.

2 Wash the rice until the water runs clear. Put the rice into a pan, pour the chicken and all the wok juices over it and mix well. Pour the water into the pan and bring to the boil, then cover the pan and simmer on a medium heat for 20 minutes.

3 Fluff up the rice and serve immediately with garlic spinach.

Ching's Tips

- Here the chicken thighs are cut in half across the bone – use a good cleaver and make sure you cut twice, aiming at the same spot, or you will end up with very small pieces of bone in your dish. Or get your butcher to do it. Alternatively, de-bone the chicken thighs – but cooking the meat with the bone in is much more flavourful.
- Do use pure sesame oil rather than toasted sesame oil – pure sesame oil provides a deeper sweet flavour.

Spicy Sichuan pepper prawn-fried rice

This is a one-pot supper dish that is easy to make and so nutritious too. It uses Sichuan peppercorns and chillies to create a numbing, tingling heat, which is then tempered by the rice.

SERVES 2

350ml/12fl oz water

150g/5oz equal mix of brown basmati long-grain rice and wild rice

1 tablespoon groundnut oil

1 teaspoon Sichuan peppercorns

5 fat garlic cloves, finely chopped

2 bird's eye chillies, deseeded and finely sliced

275g/10oz cooked tiger prawns

200g/7oz frozen edamame beans

6 ripe cherry tomatoes, halved

2 tablespoons light soy sauce

juice of 1 lime

1 small handful of fresh coriander, finely chopped

2 tablespoons chilli oil

1 Put the water and rice in a pan over a high heat and bring to the boil, then turn the heat down to low, cover the pan and simmer for 20 minutes. Once cooked, fluff up the rice with a fork and it's ready to use.

2 Heat a wok over a high heat and add the groundnut oil. When the oil starts to smoke, add the Sichuan peppercorns and stir-fry for a few seconds to help release their aroma. Add the garlic and chillies to the wok and stir-fry rapidly for a few seconds, then add the prawns and keep stirring.

3 Add the edamame beans and stir well for 1 minute, then add the cherry tomatoes and stir-fry for 30 seconds. Add the cooked rice at this stage, toss the ingredients together and cook for 1 minute.

4 Season with the soy sauce and lime juice and toss again. Add the coriander and mix in well. Transfer to serving bowls, add a drizzle of chilli oil and serve.

Taiwanese ginger & sesame chicken noodle soup

This is a Yang-yang dish (fiery chi-giving, when described in terms of traditional Chinese food philosophy) and is perfect for the winter months or on a cold day. While the mushrooms are soaking you can get on with preparing the rest of the ingredients.

SERVES 2 OR 4 TO SHARE AS A STARTER

100g/3½oz very thin dried wheat flour noodles

50ml/2fl oz toasted sesame oil (see Ching's Tip), plus extra for drizzling

1 tablespoon groundnut oil

5cm/2 inch piece of fresh root ginger, peeled and finely sliced

3 whole dried Chinese mushrooms, pre-soaked in hot water for 20 minutes, then drained

450g/1lb chicken leg quarters, with or without skin, the thigh and drumstick pieces halved on the bone

1 tablespoon Shaohsing rice wine or dry sherry

500ml/18fl oz hot chicken stock

1 tablespoon light soy sauce

2 spring onions, sliced lengthways into 7.5cm/3 inch pieces

1 pinch of salt

ground white pepper

1 Bring a pan of water to the boil. Add the wheat flour noodles, bring back to the boil and cook for 3 minutes. Drain the noodles, rinse under cold water, then drain again. Drizzle with sesame oil to prevent them from sticking together.

2 Heat a wok over a high heat and add the groundnut oil. When the oil starts to smoke, add the ginger and mushrooms and stir-fry for a few seconds until fragrant. Add the chicken and stir-fry for 1 minute until starting to turn brown, then add the rice wine or sherry. Add the hot stock, sesame oil, soy sauce, spring onions, salt and pepper and bring to the boil, then turn the heat down to medium and simmer for 10 minutes.

3 Add the cooked noodles, season further to taste with salt and serve immediately.

Ching's Tip

■ Whenever my mother made this dish the smell of sesame would fill the whole house. Mum's original recipe called for a lot more sesame oil – I have halved the quantity here, but you can adjust it to your liking.

Prep time: 15 minutes
(plus 20 minutes chilling)

Spicy wild rice salad

This healthy and mouth-wateringly good salad couldn't be easier to make. Serve on its own when you want something healthy as a main meal, or as an accompaniment to fish, shellfish or meat dishes.

SERVES 4 TO SHARE

300g/11oz cooked brown and wild rice (100g/3½oz raw rice)

½ cucumber, deseeded and finely diced

1 medium red chilli, deseeded and finely chopped

6 red radishes, finely diced

1 red pepper, deseeded and finely diced

5 tablespoons lemon juice

3 tablespoons olive oil

2 tablespoons light soy sauce

1 tablespoon toasted sesame oil

1 small handful of freshly chopped coriander

sea salt and ground black pepper

2 whole radishes to garnish

1 Mix all the ingredients for the salad together and chill for 20 minutes before serving.

2 Garnish with the radishes and serve.

Ching's Tip

- For those who love a 'bite', you can also add some freshly grated garlic or garlic purée.

Rice wine pepper beef noodles

This makes a satisfying, tasty and easy supper for two. The beef is marinated in a delicious marinade for as long as you have and then wokked-up with egg noodles and crunchy beans.

SERVES 2 AS A MAIN OR 4 TO SHARE

350g/12oz rump or sirloin steak, fat removed, cut into 5mm/¼ inch slices

200g/7oz dried yellow shi wheat flour noodles or dried egg noodles

a dash of toasted sesame oil

1 tablespoon groundnut oil

150g/5oz French beans, trimmed and sliced into thirds

1 medium red chilli, deseeded and finely chopped

200ml/7fl oz hot vegetable stock

1 tablespoon light soy sauce

1 tablespoon dark soy sauce

1 teaspoon cornflour blended with 1 tablespoon cold water

FOR THE MARINADE

2 garlic cloves, finely chopped

1 teaspoon freshly grated root ginger

1 tablespoon light soy sauce

½ teaspoon cracked black pepper (or more to taste)

1 tablespoon Shaohsing rice wine or dry sherry

1 teaspoon light brown sugar

1 teaspoon cornflour

Spicy fragrant minced pork with pickled soy 'lettuce', spinach rice

You can serve this dish any way you like – add cooked jasmine rice and mix all the ingredients together for a one-dish supper, or serve the dish on top of plain steamed rice.

SERVES 2

1 tablespoon groundnut oil

1 teaspoon Sichuan peppercorns

3 garlic cloves, crushed and finely chopped

1 tablespoon freshly grated root ginger

250g/9oz minced lean pork

1 tablespoon Shaohsing rice wine or dry sherry

2 heaped tablespoons pickled soy 'lettuce' stems, or pickled cornichons, finely chopped

1 tablespoon light soy sauce

1 teaspoon dark soy sauce

1 teaspoon Chinkiang black rice vinegar or balsamic vinegar

350g/12oz cooked jasmine rice (120g/scant 4oz raw rice, see page 154)

200g/7oz spinach leaves

a dash of toasted sesame oil

1 Heat a wok over a high heat and add the groundnut oil. When the oil starts to smoke, add the Sichuan peppercorns and toss in the oil for a few seconds, then add the garlic and ginger and stir-fry quickly for a few seconds. Tip in the minced pork and break it up with a wooden spoon.

2 As the pork starts to turn brown, add the rice wine or sherry and cook for a few more seconds. Add the pickled soy lettuce or cornichons and stir well. Season with the light and dark soy sauce and the vinegar and stir well. Turn the heat down to medium and cook for 1 minute so that all the flavours fuse together.

3 Taste and season more to your liking – the dish should be quite salty in flavour. Add the cooked rice and mix well, then add the spinach and toss until wilted slightly.

4 Add a dash of sesame oil and serve immediately.

Ching's Tip

- The star of the dish has to be the pickled soy 'lettuce'. This is available in jars in Chinese supermarkets but if you can't get hold of it, try pickled cornichons instead.

Jasmine rice

SERVES 4

350g/12oz jasmine rice, washed
until the water runs clear

600ml/1 pint water

1 Place the rice in a heavy-based saucepan and add the water. Bring to the boil, then cover with a tight-fitting lid, turn the heat down to low and cook for 15–20 minutes.

2 Uncover the pan and remove from the heat. Fluff up the grains of rice with a fork and serve immediately.

Egg-fried rice

SERVES 4

2 tablespoons groundnut oil

3 eggs, beaten

50g/2oz cooked baby shrimps

50g/2oz frozen peas

400g/14oz cooked jasmine rice
(130g/generous 4oz raw rice,
see page 154)

1–2 tablespoons light soy sauce

1 tablespoon toasted sesame oil

1–2 pinches of ground white
pepper

1 Heat a wok over a high heat and add the groundnut
   oil. Pour in the beaten eggs and leave to settle for
   1–2 minutes, then swirl the liquid egg around the wok
   and, using a wooden spoon, stir to lightly scramble it.
   Transfer to a plate and set aside.

2 Add the shrimps and frozen peas to the wok and
   stir-fry for less than 1 minute. Add the rice and mix
   well until the rice has broken down.

3 Return the scrambled eggs to the wok, season with
   soy sauce, sesame oil and white pepper to taste and
   serve immediately.

Desserts & Drinks

Mango & sago sweet soup	20 minutes (plus 30 minutes soaking, and chilling)
Duo-duo lu	5 minutes
Lychee & strawberry spring rolls with vanilla ice cream & golden syrup	18 minutes
Toasted brown rice jasmine green tea	6 minutes
Pineapple sorbet with mango coconut coulis	30 minutes (plus cooling and 2–3 hours freezing)
Skewered pineapples	20 minutes (plus 1 hour marinating)
Passionate passion fruit & mango cheesecake	20 minutes (plus 30 minutes chilling)
Lei-cha	10 minutes

Mango & sago sweet soup

One of the many popular Chinese desserts is a 'sweetened soup' or 'tien-tang'. Choose a good-quality coconut milk that is creamy as it will give a wonderful aroma and richness.

SERVES 4–6

60g/2½oz sago, pre-soaked in
  cold water for 30 minutes, then
  drained (see Ching's Tip)

30g/1¼oz rock sugar or
  1 tablespoon brown sugar

1 x 425g tin of mango slices,
  drained and puréed in a blender

125ml/4fl oz coconut milk

1 Bring 1 litre/1¾ pints water to the boil in a pan.
   Add the sago, turn the heat down and simmer for
   10 minutes, then turn off the heat and leave for
   10 minutes until the sago turns transparent. Rinse
   it in cooled boiled water from the kettle and
   drain well.

2 Put the sugar and 400ml/14fl oz water into a pan and
   bring to the boil, then simmer until the sugar has
   dissolved. Add the cooked sago, mango purée and
   coconut milk and mix well. Serve hot, or leave to cool
   at room temperature for 30 minutes, then transfer
   to the fridge and chill for 1 hour before serving.
   Delicious either way.

Ching's Tip

- Sago is a powdery starch derived from the sago
  palm and it comes in granular form in various sizes.
  When heated, the grains become small sticky 'pearls'
  that make a great basis for this sweetened coconut
  mango broth.

Duo-duo lu

Yakult in Mandarin is called 'Yang-le-duo' and 'Lu' means 'green', so the nickname for this drink became 'Duo-duo lu' because of the fusion with ice-cold green tea.

SERVES 1

4 ice cubes, roughly crushed

100ml/3½fl oz ice-cold medium-strength jasmine green tea

2 bottles of Yakult

1 teaspoon honey (optional)

1 slice of lemon

1 Place the crushed ice in a large glass or tumbler. Pour the cold green tea, Yakult and honey, if you like, into a cocktail shaker, or lidded jar, and shake well.

2 Pour over the ice, garnish with a slice of lemon and serve immediately.

Lychee & strawberry spring rolls with vanilla ice cream & golden syrup

Spring rolls are a classic Chinese dish. Here, the combination of lychees and strawberries is delicious (you could also add some raspberries if you like).

SERVES 4

8 x 14.5cm/5¾ inch square spring roll wrappers (see Ching's Tips page 164)

10 fresh lychees, chopped, or 425g tin of lychees, drained and chopped

10 strawberries, sliced

1 tablespoon cornflour blended with 2 tablespoons hot water

1 teaspoon groundnut oil

vanilla ice cream and golden syrup to serve

1 Take a spring roll wrapper and place it in front of you in the shape of a diamond. Place a chopped lychee and a few slices of strawberry across the centre of the pastry, then brush each corner with the blended cornflour. Bring the two side corners over the filling to the middle. Bring the bottom corner up over the filling and continue rolling up to the top corner. Dab the top corner with more cornflour paste and press lightly to secure the spring roll. Continue in the same way until all the wrappers are filled. Keep the leftover lychees and strawberry pieces for decorating.

2 Heat a large non-stick pan or wok over a medium heat. Add the oil and leave to melt, then place the spring rolls in the pan and fry for 1 minute until golden, then turn them over to cook the other side.

3 To serve, place two spring rolls in each small serving dish, place a scoop of vanilla ice cream on top and dress with leftover fruit pieces. Drizzle with golden syrup and serve immediately.

Pineapple sorbet with mango coconut coulis

Pineapples and mangoes are among my favourite fruits and I love the combination of the two. You can vary the amount of sugar to taste, and add some rum to the mango coulis, if you like.

SERVES 4

FOR THE SORBET

200ml/7fl oz cold water

75g/3oz caster sugar

1 large ripe pineapple

zest and juice of 1 lime

FOR THE MANGO AND COCONUT SAUCE

1 fresh mango, peeled, stoned and sliced

1 tablespoon caster sugar

100ml/3½fl oz coconut milk

4 tablespoons water

1 To make the sorbet, heat the water in a pan until boiling. Add the caster sugar and stir over a low heat until the sugar has dissolved, then remove from the heat and leave to cool at room temperature.

2 Peel and core the pineapple and roughly chop into pieces. Place in a blender and whiz until very smooth, then pour into a bowl. Add the sweetened syrup and the lime juice and mix well, then stir in the lime zest. Churn the mixture in an ice-cream machine following the manufacturer's instructions, then transfer into a freezer-proof container and freeze for 2–3 hours or overnight until ready to serve.

3 Put the mango, sugar, coconut milk and water into a blender and whiz until smooth. Pour into a bowl and chill until ready to serve.

4 To serve, pour the mango and coconut sauce over the pineapple sorbet and serve immediately.

Prep time: 15 minutes, cook in: 5 minutes
(plus 1 hour marinating)

Skewered pineapples

In summer I love cooking pineapples like this on the barbeque. The star anise gives the pineapple a slightly liquorice flavour and the syrup gives it a sticky sweetness.

SERVES 4–6

1 ripe pineapple, peeled, cored and sliced into 2cm/¾ inch chunks

FOR THE SYRUP

100ml/3½fl oz hot water

2 star anise

4 tablespoons brown sugar

1 teaspoon ground cinnamon

zest and juice of 1 lime

zest and juice of 1 orange

1 Put all the ingredients for the syrup into a pan and heat until the sugar has dissolved. Add the pineapple chunks to the syrup and place in the fridge for 1 hour. Meanwhile, soak 7–8 bamboo skewers in cold water for 15 minutes.

2 When ready to cook, slide about 5 chunks of pineapple onto each skewer. Heat a griddle pan or barbecue on a high heat, then cook the pineapple skewers for 4–5 minutes, basting frequently with the syrup, until the pineapple has a delicious sticky caramel coating. Serve immediately.

Ching's Tip

- You can also skewer the pineapples onto some long pieces of lemongrass – they give off an amazing fragrance. Remove any brown outer leaves and trim the end before skewering.

Easy Entertaining

Sichuan spicy pork & prawn wontons in Sichuan chilli oil	45 minutes
Duck spring rolls	45 minutes (plus 20 minutes marinating, 10 minutes resting)
Pork & water chestnut dumplings	24–25 minutes (plus 20 minutes soaking)
Yellow bean & honey roast chicken	1¾ hours (plus overnight marinating)
Peking duck	1 hour 50 minutes (plus overnight marinating)
Sichuan chilli roast beef	45–60 minutes (plus 1 hour resting)
Lobster in hot garlic spinach sauce	30 minutes (plus 30 minutes freezing)
Aromatic beef noodle soup	1¼ hours (plus 20 minutes soaking)
Lobster in black bean beer sauce	30 minutes (plus 30 minutes freezing)
Hainanese chicken rice	2¼ hours (plus 1 hour cooling and chilling)
Sichuan chilli bean beef stew	2 hours 5 minutes
Tang yuan with sweet red bean soup	2 hours 10 minutes
Orange & green tea loaf cake	2 hours 10 minutes (plus 15 minutes cooling)

Sichuan spicy pork & prawn wontons in Sichuan chilli oil

This is my favourite way to cook wontons, laced with chilli oil and a Sichuan pepper chilli paste. You can make these fiery addictive dumplings in advance, then freeze them and cook straight from frozen when required. Perfect for that emergency dinner or for easy entertaining.

SERVES 6 AS A STARTER

36 wonton wrappers, 7.5cm/3 inch
   square

1 egg, beaten

FOR THE FILLING

200g/7oz minced pork

200g/7oz raw tiger prawns, shelled,
   deveined and finely chopped

1 large spring onion, finely
   chopped

1 tablespoon freshly grated
   root ginger

1 tablespoon light soy sauce

1 tablespoon Shaohsing rice wine
   or dry sherry

1 teaspoon toasted sesame oil

2 teaspoons cornflour

1 pinch of ground white pepper

FOR THE SESAME VINEGAR SOY DRESSING

2 tablespoons light soy sauce

2 tablespoons clear rice vinegar or
   cider vinegar

2 tablespoons toasted sesame oil

1 teaspoon toasted sesame seeds

FOR THE SICHUAN CHILLI SAUCE

4 tablespoons chilli oil

1 tablespoon light soy sauce

1 teaspoon dry-toasted Sichuan
   peppercorns, ground (see page 39)

1 teaspoon chilli sauce

TO SERVE

1 small handful of freshly
   chopped coriander

1 spring onion, sliced

1 Combine all the ingredients for the soy dressing and place in a small bowl. Do the same for the Sichuan chilli sauce. Put all the ingredients for the filling into a bowl and mix well.

2 Take one wonton wrapper and place 1½ teaspoons of the filling in the centre. Brush each side of the wrapper with the beaten egg and then gather up the sides and mould around the filling into a ball shape, twisting the top to secure. Repeat with the remaining wrappers.

3 Bring a very large pan of water to the boil over a high heat, then turn the heat down to medium and, using a slotted spoon, gently lower the dumplings into the water and cook for 5 minutes (8–9 minutes if cooking from frozen) until the skin turns translucent yellow and the wontons float lightly to the surface of the water (don't overcook them as they will open up). Test one to see if the filling is cooked. If not serving immediately, turn the heat to very low until ready. Then, using the slotted spoon, gently lift the wontons out and divide between six bowls. Spoon 1 tablespoon of the water the dumplings were cooked in over them (this keeps them moist and also dilutes the hot fiery paste and helps create a lovely sauce).

4 Serve with the dishes of chopped coriander and spring onion, the sesame vinegar soy dressing and Sichuan chilli sauce. Guests can help themselves to the dressing or sauce of their choice (or even both!).

Ching's Tips

- You can serve this as a starter or accompanied by a host of other dishes.
- If you are feeding fewer people, you can freeze the surplus wontons. For a delicious soup, cook the frozen wontons as above in vegetable stock with Chinese leaves, seasoned with light soy sauce, clear rice vinegar or cider vinegar and spring onions. Or you can make them open-wrapped and then steam them for a version of the classic Cantonese 'sui mai' dumpling.

Peking duck

This is my version of Peking duck – one I have adapted to make at home. I have also made my own Peking duck sauce to accompany the dish.

SERVES 8, MAKES ABOUT 24 PANCAKES

1 medium duck

2 litres/3½ pints boiling
water

FOR THE GLAZE

5 tablespoons clear honey

2 tablespoons dark soy sauce

4 tablespoons Chinese five-spice
  powder

2 tablespoons brown sugar

FOR THE PEKING DUCK SAUCE

2 tablespoons sesame oil

6 tablespoons hoisin sauce

6 tablespoons caster sugar

6 tablespoons water

1 tablespoon dark soy sauce

1 tablespoon cornflour blended with
  1 tablespoon cold water

TO SERVE

24 wheat flour pancakes
  (see Ching's Tip, page 189)

1 cucumber, deseeded and sliced
  lengthways into long thin strips

3 spring onions, sliced lengthways
  into long thin strips strips

1 Place the duck on a rack over a roasting tin and pour the boiling water over it. Discard the water and pat the duck dry with absorbent kitchen paper.

2 Mix together all the ingredients for the glaze and brush over the duck, inside and out. Leave to dry and glaze for about 10 minutes, then brush again. Repeat, using most of the marinade but reserve 4–5 tablespoons. Ideally, leave the duck, uncovered, in the fridge overnight to allow the glaze to settle.

3 Preheat the oven to 200°C/400°F/gas mark 6. Place the duck on a rack in a roasting tin, transfer to the oven and cook for 45 minutes. Turn the duck over and brush with the reserved marinade. Check that the bird is not getting too dark, then cook for a further 40–45 minutes or until the skin is crisp. Remove the duck on its rack from the oven, cover loosely and leave to rest. Carefully pour off the duck fat into a heatproof container.

4 To make the sauce, heat a pan or wok and add all the ingredients for the sauce except the blended cornflour. When the sauce starts to bubble slightly, add the blended cornflour and stir well to thicken. Set aside and leave to cool.

5 Oil the base of a small bamboo steamer and half-fill with wheat flour pancakes. Place the steamer over a pan of boiling water (making sure the water does not touch the base of the steamer), cover with the lid and steam for 3–4 minutes until the pancakes are soft and cooked. Repeat with the remaining pancakes.

6 Carve and slice some duck. Place a teaspoon of the sauce on a pancake, top with some of the duck meat, cucumber and spring onions, roll up and serve immediately. Repeat with the remaining pancakes.

Ching's Tip

- The wheat flour pancakes are a must and can be bought from any Chinese supermarket. Buy a large batch and then store in your freezer for whenever you need them.

Sichuan chilli roast beef

I love English roast beef with all the trimmings, so I decided to try a different style of roast beef with one of my favourite ingredients – Sichuan peppercorns. This Chinese-style roast is great served with garlic spinach, mixed vegetable stir-fry and roasted sweet potatoes (and of course you can serve it with gravy too).

SERVES 4–5

1.3kg/2¾lb beef rib or sirloin joint on the bone (see Ching's Tips)

plain flour

2 tablespoons crushed Sichuan peppercorns

1 tablespoon Chinese five-spice powder

1 teaspoon dried red chilli flakes

3 medium shallots, halved

300ml/10fl oz hot beef stock

sea salt and cracked black pepper

garlic spinach (see page 122) and roast sweet potatoes to serve

1 Preheat the oven to 240°C/475°F/gas mark 9. Place the beef on a board and season the fat with 1 tablespoon flour, the crushed Sichuan peppercorns, five-spice powder, chilli flakes, salt and black pepper. Place the shallots in a roasting tin and put the beef on top.

2 Roast in the oven for 20 minutes, then turn the heat down to 190°C/375°F/gas mark 5 and cook for a further 20 minutes for rare, 35 minutes for medium, longer for well done. (As a guideline, it takes 15 minutes to cook the meat for every 450g/1lb.) During the cooking time, remove the beef from the oven about three times and baste it with its juices so you get really delicious meat (keep the oven door closed while basting so as not to lower the temperature).

3 Insert a metal skewer into the meat to make sure it is cooked to your preference – check whether the colour of the meat juice runs red, pink or clear. Then cover with foil and leave to stand for at least 1 hour before serving so that the meat relaxes.

4   When you are ready to serve, make the gravy. Transfer the meat to a plate, then pour all the juices from the roasting tin into a pan and, using a tablespoon, skim off any fat. Stir in some flour and, stirring very quickly and continuously, add the hot stock a little at a time until you get the right consistency.

5   To serve, carve the roast beef into medium slices and serve with garlic spinach, roast sweet potatoes and the gravy.

Ching's Tips

■ If you can afford to be extravagant, buy a sirloin joint on the bone; or for everyday cooking, use a rib joint. Make sure you keep the fat on because it keeps the meat lovely and moist whilst cooking.

■ You can slice any leftover beef into thin slices and make the Roast beef in 'four-spiced' chilli oil (see page 74), or cold roast beef and mustard sandwiches.

Prep time: 15 minutes, cook in: 15 minutes
(plus 30 minutes freezing)

Lobster in hot garlic spinach sauce

This is finger-lickingly good and also healthy and delicious. Serve it as a main dish to share with egg-fried rice or add yellow shi wheat flour or egg noodles to the cooked lobster for a noodle dish.

SERVES 2

1 medium-size live lobster

1 x 220g tin of crabmeat in brine, drained

1 tablespoon light soy sauce

sea salt

egg-fried rice to serve
  (see page 155)

FOR THE SAUCE

1 tablespoon groundnut oil

3 garlic cloves, crushed

1 medium red chilli, deseeded and finely chopped

1 large bunch of fresh coriander

1 large handful of spinach

1 Prepare the live lobster by placing it in the freezer for 30 minutes.

2 Heat a large pan of water until boiling. Quickly plunge the lobster into the water and cook for 8 minutes or until the lobster has turned completely pink. Lift out and drain well. (You can use the lobster broth for a seafood soup.)

3 Using a large cleaver or knife, chop off the tail and cut into three sections. Pull off the claws. Using the back of the cleaver, crack the shell of the claws and all the lobster pieces – this helps to let the sauce seep into the lobster and flavour the meat when cooking. Divide the body of the lobster in half lengthways and then spoon out the brown flesh, if preferred, and discard. Chop each half into two pieces.

4 Put all the ingredients for the sauce in a blender with 200ml/7fl oz lobster broth and whiz until smooth.

5 Heat a wok over a high heat. Pour in the sauce, add the crabmeat and season to taste with soy sauce. Bring the sauce to a simmer, then toss the lobster pieces into the sauce, mix well and cook for 1–2 minutes. Take off the heat and serve immediately with egg-fried rice.

Aromatic beef noodle soup

This is a more-ish beef noodle soup, easy to cook and perfect for entertaining on a cold winter's day.

**SERVES 2 AS A MAIN
OR 4 AS A STARTER**

FOR THE SOUP

350g/12oz stewing beef

1 litre/1¾ pints water

3 garlic cloves, finely chopped

2.5cm/1 inch piece of fresh root
  ginger, peeled and sliced

2 cinnamon sticks

3 star anise

3 whole dried Chinese mushrooms,
  pre-soaked in hot water for
  20 minutes, then drained

50ml/2fl oz light soy sauce

50ml/2fl oz Shaohsing rice wine
  or dry sherry

2 tablespoons brown sugar

TO SERVE

200g/7oz flat udon or wheat flour
  noodles

toasted sesame oil

200g/7oz pak choy leaves, trimmed,
  separated and chopped

2 large spring onions, finely sliced

1 small handful of fresh coriander

chilli oil and chilli sauce (optional)

1 Heat a pan over a medium heat and add all the
ingredients for the soup, then turn the heat up to
high, cover the pan and bring to the boil. Turn the
heat down to medium, uncover the pan and cook for
1 hour until the beef is tender and fragrant.

2 Towards the end of the cooking time, cook the
noodles in a pan of boiling water for 3 minutes. Drain,
rinse under cold water and drain again, then drizzle
with sesame oil to prevent the noodles from sticking
together.

3 Place the pak choy leaves on a heatproof plate and
put into a bamboo steamer. Cover with a lid and place
over a pan of boiling water (making sure the water
does not touch the base of the steamer). Steam on a
high heat for 3–4 minutes until the leaves have wilted
and the stems are cooked.

4 Divide the noodles between serving bowls and put
some pak choy leaves, spring onions and chopped
coriander into each. Ladle the soup and beef pieces
into the bowls, drizzle with more sesame oil or chilli
oil and chilli sauce, if you like, and serve immediately.

Hainanese chicken rice

This dish is one of Singapore's national favourites. If serving just two people, you can also use chicken thighs on the bone instead of a whole chicken, just adjust the recipe quantities using your own judgement.

SERVES 4

2.7kg/6lb whole chicken

2 teaspoons salt

5cm/2 inch piece of fresh root ginger, peeled and sliced

2 white onions, finely chopped

4 tablespoons Shaohsing rice wine or dry sherry

200g/7oz jasmine rice

200ml/7fl oz water

FOR THE SOUP

1 tablespoon groundnut oil

2 small shallots, finely chopped

2 medium red chillies, deseeded and chopped

2 red tomatoes, chopped

½ cucumber, peeled, halved, deseeded and sliced into crescents 1cm/½ inch thick

FOR THE GARLIC GINGER SAUCE

4 tablespoons groundnut oil

3 garlic cloves, minced

1 tablespoon freshly grated root ginger

2 tablespoons reserved chicken stock

salt and ground white pepper

FOR THE CHILLI, CORIANDER & SPRING ONION SAUCE

2 garlic cloves, finely chopped

1 tablespoon freshly grated root ginger

2 medium red chillies, deseeded and roughly chopped

2 tablespoons light soy sauce

2 tablespoons clear rice vinegar or cider vinegar

1 tablespoon toasted sesame oil

1 pinch of salt

1 pinch of caster sugar

1 spring onion, finely chopped

1 small handful of freshly chopped coriander

1 Wash the chicken, giblets and neck (if available) under cold running water and pat dry. Smear the salt over the chicken, inside and out. Put the chicken, ginger, onions and rice wine or sherry into a large wok or casserole dish with enough water to cover the chicken. Partially cover the wok or dish, bring the ingredients to a gentle simmer over a medium heat and cook for 45 minutes. Turn the chicken over and simmer for another 45 minutes.

2 When the chicken is cooked, carefully remove from the stock (reserving the stock) and leave until cool enough to handle. Chop the chicken into bite-size/serving pieces and place on a large platter or plate, then cover with foil and leave at room temperature until ready to serve.

3 Cool the stock for 30 minutes at room temperature, then refrigerate it for 30 minutes. Skim the fat off the surface of the stock and pass through a sieve to give a fine texture.

4 Meanwhile, wash the rice until the water runs clear, then place in a pan with the water and 250ml/9fl oz of the stock (reserve the remaining stock – there should be about 800ml/1 pint 7fl oz). Bring to the boil, then cover the pan, turn the heat down to low and cook for 15–20 minutes until fluffy.

5 Put all the ingredients for the garlic ginger sauce into a pestle and mortar and crush, then transfer to a small bowl. Do the same for the chilli, coriander and spring onion sauce. Set both aside until needed.

6 To make the soup, heat another wok on a high heat and add the groundnut oil. When the oil starts to smoke, add the shallots and stir-fry until translucent. Then add the chillies, tomatoes and cucumber and pour in the remaining chicken stock. Stir well and bring to the boil.

7 To serve, place the chicken on a platter and serve with the two sauces, small dishes of the soup and a bowl of rice each.

Sichuan chilli bean beef stew

This is one of my favourite Chinese stews of all time. It is also the basis for a good noodle soup and you can add potatoes if you like. What makes this dish delicious is a good-quality chilli bean sauce — try to buy a Chinese brand from a Chinese supermarket.

SERVES 4–6

2 garlic cloves, crushed

2.5cm/1 inch piece of fresh root ginger, peeled and sliced

1 red chilli, deseeded and chopped

1 onion, sliced

2 medium carrots, cut into 2cm/¾ inch thick slices

1kg/2¼lb braising beef (see Ching's Tips)

1 litre/1¾ pints vegetable stock

2 tablespoons chilli bean paste

1 tablespoon light soy sauce

1 teaspoon dark soy sauce

2 teaspoons brown sugar

2 tablespoons cornflour blended with 2 tablespoons cold water (optional)

1 spring onion, sliced

1 small handful of fresh coriander, sliced

sweet potato jasmine rice (see page 137) or steamed jasmine rice (see page 154) to serve

1 Put all the ingredients except the blended cornflour, spring onion and coriander into a large pan and bring to the boil. Turn the heat down to low, cover the pan and simmer for 2 hours.

2 Once it's cooked, thicken the broth, if you like, by stirring in the blended cornflour.

3 Garnish with the spring onion and coriander and serve over sweet potato jasmine rice or jasmine rice.

Ching's Tips

- I suggest using a good-quality braising beef or beef shank because the meat is cooked on a simmering heat for 2 hours, after which it becomes delightfully meltingly tender.
- You can also serve with wheat flour noodles: cook and drain them and place in serving bowls, then pour the broth over to make a delicious noodle soup (you won't need to add the blended cornflour).

Tang yuan with sweet red bean soup

This is a classic Chinese dessert eaten on many festivals and traditional occasions. Best served hot, but it is also refreshing cold, when the dumplings tend to be firmer. The texture of the dumplings is delightfully sticky, light and tender. Enjoy!

SERVES 8–10

about 1.6 litres/2¾ pints water
140g/4½oz glutinous rice flour
100g/3½oz rock sugar

FOR THE BEANS
1 litre/1¾ pints water
200g/7oz adzuki red beans,
   washed and drained
   (see Ching's Tips)

1 To cook the beans, bring the water to the boil and add the beans. Cover the pan and cook on a low–medium heat for 75 minutes until soft. Check from time to time that there is enough water in the pan and top up with boiling water if necessary. Drain the beans and put to one side.

2 To make the dumplings, mix 100ml/3½fl oz of the water with the rice flour and knead into a dough. Take a small piece of dough and roll in your palm into a small round ball about 1.5cm/⅔ inch in diameter. Make 50 similar-size balls.

3 Bring the remaining 1.5 litres/2½ pints water to the boil. Add the rock sugar and leave to dissolve. Add the dumplings and cook until they float to the surface, then ladle the cooked red beans into the pan, stir well and serve immediately.

Ching's Tips

- You can pre-soak the beans overnight if you've time, in which case the cooking time will be reduced by 20 minutes.
- If you prefer, you can use canned adzuki beans – 4 x 410g cans. Drain well and add to the boiling water at step 3 with the rock sugar.
- Some traditional variations also add a few slices of ginger to the sweetened broth.

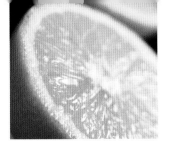

Orange & green tea loaf cake

This is one of my favourite cake recipes and it has the fabulous light taste of ground almonds. For a slight bitter sweetness, I have added some crushed fine jasmine green tea leaves.

SERVES 4

700ml/1 pint 3½fl oz water

1 large ripe orange, washed thoroughly

FOR THE CAKE MIXTURE

1 teaspoon butter to grease

1 teaspoon plain flour to dust

3 medium eggs

125g/4oz ground almonds

125g/4oz caster sugar

1 teaspoon jasmine green tea leaves

zest of 1 large ripe orange

1 tablespoon baking powder

1 Pour the water into a pan and bring to the boil. Lower the orange into the pan and cook on a medium heat, gently boiling, for 1 hour. Once the orange is cooked, leave to cool, then slice into quarters and remove any pips. Transfer to a food processor and blend well.

2 To make the cake, butter and flour a 19cm/7½ inch long, 9cm/7½ inch wide, 9.5cm/3¾ inch high loaf tin. Preheat the oven to 180°C/350°F/gas mark 4.

3 Beat the eggs in a bowl, then stir in the orange pulp with all the remaining ingredients. Pour into the loaf tin and cook for 50 minutes–1 hour, until the cake is golden and has risen and a skewer inserted into the centre comes out clean.

4 Leave the cake to cool in the tin for about 15 minutes. When the cake has cooled, carefully remove it from the tin, cut into thick slices and serve with clotted cream and toasted brown rice jasmine green tea (see page 165).

Ching's Tips

■ You can double the quantity and bake an even larger cake so that you have plenty to keep for afternoon tea, because there is nothing more uplifting than a large slice of this cake for tea. Depending on the size of your cake tin, it might take 8–10 minutes longer to cook.

■ As an alternative to clotted cream, serve this with frozen lime yoghurt – delicious!

Ching's Menus

You may have to adjust the quantities in some of the recipes below to fit the number of guests you are feeding. I always tend to cook a little more so that people can either have seconds or I can turn the leftovers into something exciting the next day...

Traditional Chinese New Year party for 6–8

Starter
Sweet and sour Wuxi ribs (page 20)
Grandma's pork and golden needle soup (page 8)
Duck spring rolls (page 180)
Sichuan spicy pork and prawn wontons in Sichuan chilli oil (page 177)
Pork and water chestnut dumplings (page 182)

Second course
Peking duck (page 187)

Main course
Steamed wine sea bass (page 82)
Lobster in black bean beer sauce (page 196)
Razor clams with lardons and bamboo shoots (page 99)
Rice wine tomato king prawns (page 106)

Accompaniments
Egg and tomato spring onion stir-fry (page 123)
Shanghai-style crabmeat and egg noodle (page 136)
Mum's sweet potato jasmine rice (page 137)

Tea
Toasted brown rice jasmine green tea (page 165, increase the quantities accordingly)

Dessert
Tang yuan with sweet red bean soup (page 202)

Modern Western-style Chinese New Year party for 4

Starter
Crabmeat sweetcorn soup with black truffle (page 10)

Main course
Spicy bacon crispy haddock (page 89)

Dessert
Lychee and strawberry spring rolls with vanilla ice cream and golden syrup (page 163)

Easy entertaining – Chinese buffet for 8
(make double the quantities as necessary)

Starter
Traditional-style hot and sour soup (page 5)
Sichuan-style style sweet and sour prawns (page 109)
Sichuan spicy pork and prawn wontons in Sichuan chilli oil (page 177)

Main course
Yellow bean & honey roast chicken (page 184)
Sichuan chilli bean beef stew (page 201)
Steamed wine sea bass (page 82)

Accompaniments
Spicy red cabbage and edamame beans (page 128)
Garlic spinach (page 122)
Egg-fried rice (page 155)

Dessert
Skewered pineapples (page 168)

Easy entertaining – Dinner for 6

Starter
Traditional-style hot and sour soup (page 5)
Peking duck (page 187) – or serve as a separate course

Main course

Sichuan chilli roast beef (page 190, you will need to buy a larger piece of beef)

Accompaniments

Garlic pak choy exotic mushroom stir-fry (page 127)
Garlic spinach (page 122)
Mum's sweet potato jasmine rice (page 137)

Dessert

Passionate passion fruit and mango cheesecake (page 170, make double the quantity and have enough for seconds)

Easy entertaining – Dinner for 4 to share

Starter

Yellow bean scallops and chives (page 13)
Citrusy salad (page 131)

Main course

Hot pink pepper/black pepper chicken (page 51)
Spicy bacon crispy haddock (page 89)
Saucy beef dofu (page 73)
Chongqing beef (page 72)

Accompaniments

Mum's sweet potato jasmine rice (page 137)
Garlic spinach (page 122)

Dessert

Lychee and strawberry spring rolls with vanilla ice cream and golden syrup (page 163)

Easy entertaining – Special seafood dinner for 2

Starter

Sea bass and dofu clear soup (page 7, halve the quantity)
Wok-fried crispy scallops (page 15)

Main course

Sweet and smoky 'hong sao yu' (page 92)

Accompaniments

Garlic spinach (page 122)
Garlic pak choy exotic mushroom stir-fry (page 127)

Dessert

Pineapple sorbet with mango coconut coulis (page 167, keep any leftover sorbet in the freezer)

Easy entertaining – Special seafood and meat dinner for 2

Starter

Yellow bean scallops and chives (page 13)

Main course

Garlic chilli pepper beef and mushroom pak choy (page 76)

Accompaniments

Garlic spinach (page 122)
Jasmine rice (page 154)

Dessert

Orange and green tea loaf cake (page 205)

One-pot nutritious light soup meals

Shrimp, crabmeat, dofu and spinach soup (page 11)
Grandfather's egg, mixed mushroom and celery broth (page 12)
Crabmeat sweetcorn soup with black truffle (page 10)
Sea bass and dofu clear soup (page 7)
Grandma's pork and golden needle soup (page 8)

One-wok healthy quick meals

Oriental mushrooms and dofu in garlic black bean sauce (page 120)
Spicy Sichuan pepper prawn-fried rice (page 142)
Rice wine pepper beef noodles (page 149)
Spicy fragrant minced pork with pickled soy 'lettuce', spinach rice (page 152)
Spicy Sichuan aubergine (page 119)
Chilli bean cod (page 84)
Dofu ru haddock (page 83)
Ginger, chilli and soy-steamed cod (page 90)
Sweet and sour monkfish fillets (page 86)
Sweet and smoky 'hong sao yu' (page 92)
Chicken and snake bean stir-fry (page 44)
Chicken and black bean stir-fry (page 47)
Sweet and sour duck (page 48)
Hot pink pepper/black pepper chicken (page 51)
Cold spicy chicken salad with hot dressing (page 56)
Steamed chicken with sour and spicy dressing and spinach (page 52)

One-course casual entertaining dinners

Sichuan chilli bean beef stew (page 201), served with Mum's sweet potato jasmine rice (page 137)
Aromatic beef noodle soup (page 194)
Taiwanese ginger and sesame chicken noodle soup (page 144)
Mixed seafood crispy noodle (page 139)
Chicken rice (page 141), served with Garlic spinach (page 122)

Vegetarian dinner for 4

Starter

Lotus root crisps (page 125)
Spicy red cabbage and edamame beans (page 128)
Traditional-style hot and sour soup (omit the chicken) (page 5)

Main course

Spicy Sichuan aubergine (page 119)
Oriental mushrooms and dofu in garlic black bean sauce (page 120)
Egg and tomato spring onion stir-fry (page 123)

Accompaniments

Garlic spinach (page 122)
Mum's sweet potato jasmine rice (page 137)

Dessert

Passionate passion fruit and mango cheesecake (page 170)

Afternoon tea

Lei-cha (page 171)
Toasted brown rice jasmine green tea (page 165)
Orange and green tea loaf cake (page 205)

Afternoon tea for children

Duo-duo lu (page 161)
Orange and green tea loaf cake (page 205)

Sunday lunch for 4

Starter

Sweet and sour Wuxi ribs (page 20, make double the quantity)

Main course

Yellow bean and honey roast chicken (page 184, with enough for seconds)

Accompaniments

Citrusy salad (page 131)
Spicy red cabbage (page 126)
Garlic pak choy exotic mushroom stir-fry (page 127)
Spicy wild rice salad (page 146)

Dessert

Skewered pineapples (page 168)

Easy entertaining for friends for 4

Starter

Sweet and sour Wuxi ribs (page 20)
Fried sweet chilli chicken (page 54)
Breaded haddock with Sichuan pepper, chilli and salt (page 91)
Cantonese-style sweet and sour pork (page 30)

Main course

Cantonese-style duck with rice (page 151, make double the quantity)

Dessert

Pineapple sorbet with mango coconut coulis (page 167)

For a cocktail dim sum party – choose 6–8 dishes for 6–8 people

Crabmeat sweetcorn soup with black truffle (page 10)
Wok-fried crispy scallops (page 15)
Century duck eggs with coriander and mushroom sauce (page 19)
Sweet and sour Wuxi ribs (page 20)
Butter batter prawns (page 18)
Breaded haddock with Sichuan pepper, chilli and salt (page 91)
Sichuan spicy pork and prawns wontons in Sichuan chilli oil (page 177)
Duck spring rolls (page 180)
Pork and water chestnut dumplings (page 182)
Peking duck (page 187)
Fried sweet chilli chicken (page 54)
Three-cup chicken (page 57)
Sweet and sour duck (page 48)
Hot pink pepper/black pepper chicken (page 51)
Steamed chicken with sour and spicy dressing and spinach (page 52)
Lotus root crisps (page 125)
Spicy red cabbage and edamame beans (page 128)
Crispy Mongolian lamb (page 68)
Spicy chunky lamb (page 71)
Roast beef in 'four-spiced' chilli oil (page 75)

Lychee and strawberry spring rolls with vanilla
ice cream and golden syrup (page 163)
Skewered pineapples (page 168)
Mango and sago sweet soup (page 160)
Chicken rice 'Bi-ge' (page 141)
Taiwan-inspired 'teriyaki' squid (page 113)
Exploding river prawns (page 100)
Wok-fried octopus with garlic coriander salsa
(page 104)

Takeaway-themed dinner for 4 – choose from:

Starter

Traditional-style hot and sour soup (page 5)
Crabmeat sweetcorn soup with black truffle
(page 10)
Butter batter prawns (page 18)
Sweet and sour Wuxi ribs (page 20)
Sichuan spicy pork and prawn wontons in
Sichuan chilli oil (page 177)
Duck spring rolls (page 180)
Peking duck (page 187)

Main course

Sweet and sour monkfish fillets (page 86)
Chicken and black bean stir-fry (page 47)
Sweet and sour duck (page 48)
Hot pink pepper/black pepper chicken
(page 51)
Fried sweet chilli chicken (page 54)
Juicy chilli chicken and cashew nut (page 60)
Curry chicken stir-fry (page 62)
Garlic chilli pepper beef and mushroom
pak choy (page 76)
Mixed seafood crispy noodle (page 139)
Cantonese-style duck with rice (page 151)
Cantonese-style sweet and sour pork
(page 30)
Egg-fried rice (page 155)

Dessert

Lychee and strawberry spring rolls with vanilla
ice cream with golden syrup (page 163)

Chilli-themed dinner for 4 – choose from:

Starter

Traditional-style hot and sour soup (page 5)
Sichuan spicy pork and prawn wontons in
Sichuan chilli oil (page 177)
Roast beef in 'four-spiced' chilli oil (page 75)

Main course

Chilli bean cod (page 84)
Ginger, chilli and soy-steamed cod
(page 90)
Sichuan chilli roast beef (page 190)
Juicy chilli chicken and cashew nut
(page 60)
Steamed chicken with sour and spicy dressing
and spinach (page 52)
Chongqing beef (page 72)
Spicy Sichuan pepper prawn-fried rice
(page 142)
Spicy wild rice salad (page 146)
Prawn and chilli bamboo shoot stir-fry
(page 111)
Sichuan-style sweet and sour prawns
(page 109)
Squid and crevettes in chilli tomato sauce
(page 107)
Spicy red cabbage and edamame beans
(page 128)

Dessert

Pineapple sorbet with mango coconut coulis
(page 167)

Seafood themed dinner for 4–6 to share

Starter

Shrimp, crabmeat, dofu and spinach soup
(page 11)
Wok-fried crispy scallops (page 15)
Yellow bean scallops and chives (page 13)
Sichuan-style sweet and sour prawns
(page 109)

Main course

Steamed wine sea bass (page 82)
Lobster in hot garlic spinach sauce
(page 193)
Exploding river prawns (page 100)
Rice wine tomato king prawns (page 106)
Razor clams with lardons and bamboo shoots
(page 99)

Accompaniments

Spicy wild rice salad (page 146)
Citrusy salad (page 131)
Jasmine rice (page 154)
Garlic spinach (page 122)

Dessert

Pineapple sorbet with mango coconut coulis
(page 167)

The store cupboard

My top ten essential Chinese store cupboard ingredients:

1 Light soy sauce
2 Dark soy sauce
3 Shaohsing rice wine
4 Toasted sesame oil
5 Five-spice powder
6 Sichuan peppercorns
7 Chinkiang black rice vinegar
8 Clear rice vinegar
9 Chilli bean sauce
10 Chilli sauce

My favourite ingredients for making sauces:

Chilli oil
Fermented salted black beans
Oyster sauce
Hoisin sauce
Yellow bean sauce

Important flavourings:

Garlic
Fresh root ginger
Coriander
Spring onions
Chillies

Suitable oils:

Groundnut oil or vegetable oil

Other specialist ingredients:

Dried Chinese mushrooms
Dried baby shrimps
Dried tangerine peel
Dried chilli flakes
Dried Sichuan chillies
Cinnamon stick/bark
Fennel
Cloves
Star anise
Jasmine rice

Glossary

Unless otherwise stated, the ingredient should be available in most high-street supermarkets.

Adzuki red bean/red bean paste (tinned)
These are whole red beans the size of small oblong-shaped pearls. They are high in protein. Cooked adzuki red beans, in tins, are available from most supermarkets. Sweet ready-prepared red bean paste, available from Chinese supermarkets, is a popular Chinese dessert filling.

Bamboo shoots (tinned)
Drain tinned bamboo shoots and use them in stir-fries and soups. They are rarely available fresh.

Black rice vinegar – see Chinkiang black rice vinegar

Century eggs (preserved)
These are duck eggs (sometimes called thousand-year-old eggs) that have been buried in salt, tea leaves and rice husk, covered with sodium bicarbonate and left to mature for 40–50 days. The yolk has a rich creamy texture and, when served chilled, the white is clear, jelly-like and fragrant. Do not confuse these with preserved salted duck eggs – matured for 20 days, they have a deep orange yolk and an opaque clean white.

Chilli bean paste (sauce)
Mainly used in Sichuan cooking, this is made from broad beans and chillies that have been fermented with salt to give a deep brown-red

sauce. Some versions include fermented soya beans or garlic. This makes a great stewing sauce but use with caution, as some varieties are extremely hot.

Chilli oil (oil)
This is made from dried red chillies heated in oil to give a spicy orange-red fiery oil. Some chilli oils also contain specks of dried chillies. Available from any Chinese super-market or you can make your own: heat a wok over a medium heat and add some groundnut oil. Add dried chilli flakes with seeds and heat for 2 minutes. Take off the heat and leave the chilli flakes to infuse in the oil until the oil has completely cooled. Decant into a glass jar with a tight lid and store for a month before using. For a clear oil, pass through a sieve.

Chilli sauce (ingredient/dipping sauce)
This can be used in cooking or as a dipping sauce. There are several varieties; some are flavoured with garlic and vinegar. For sweet chilli sauce I use the Mae Ploy brand.

Chinese beer
Use a light, clear beer, not too strong. Great for drinking and cooking. Alternatively, use a mild lager.

Chinese black truffle (fresh)
This winter truffle harvested in China has an earthy mushroom pungency and tastes nutty. It is often used as a substitute for the more expensive variety of

European/French truffles, and can be used in the same way, grated or added into savoury dishes.

Chinese broccoli – see Chinese kale

Chinese cabbage (fresh)
Also known as Napa cabbage, Tianjin cabbage or Chinese leaf, it has a delicate sweet aroma with a mild cabbage flavour that disappears when the vegetable is cooked. The white stalk has a crunchy texture and remains succulent even after prolonged cooking. The Koreans mainly use it in their pickled cabbage dish called kimchee.

Chinese chives – see Garlic chives

Chinese five-spice powder (spice)
This is a blend of cinnamon, cloves, Sichuan peppercorns, fennel and star anise. These five spices give the sour, bitter, pungent, sweet and salty flavours in Chinese cooking. This spice works very well with meats and in marinades.

Chinese wood ear mushrooms (dried)
These dark brown-black fungi have ear-shaped caps and are very crunchy in texture. They do not impart flavour but add colour and crispness to any dish. They should be soaked in hot water for 20 minutes before cooking – they will double in size. After soaking they should be rinsed well to remove any dirt. Store the dried pieces in a glass jar and seal tightly. Available from Chinese supermarkets.

scrambled eggs, pickled turnip, salted peanuts, fermented bean curd (dofu ru), pickled cucumbers and chilli-pickled bamboo shoots.

Coriander (fresh)

This is mainly used as a garnish or in soups, stir-fries, stews and cold tossed salads. Both the leaves and stems are used.

Coriander seeds (spice)

The dried seeds of the coriander herb. When ground, they give a distinctive warm citrusy aroma to sweet and savoury dishes.

Cumin (spice)

This is the dried seed of the herb *Cuminum cyminum*, and belongs to the parsley family. When ground it has a distinctive, slightly bitter but warm flavour.

Curry powder (spice)

There are many different blends of curry powder. As well as Chinese five-spice powder, some also include coriander, turmeric, cumin, ginger and garlic.

Daikon or white radish (fresh)

This grows in the ground like a root vegetable, and resembles a large white carrot. It has a peppery and crunchy taste and can be eaten raw, pickled or cooked. Daikon contains vitamin C and diastase, an enzyme that helps digestion. It can be sliced or shredded and added to soups, salads and stir-fries. The Koreans use this vegetable to make kimchee, their famous pickle. Store in a sealed bag – daikon has a pungent smell.

Dark soy sauce (condiment)

Made from wheat and fermented soya beans, dark soy sauce has been aged a lot longer than the light soy variety. It is mellower

and less salty in taste than light soy, and is used to give flavour and colour.

Deep-fried dofu (bean curd) (fresh)

This is fresh bean curd that has been deep-fried to a golden brown to make it crispy and crunchy on the outside. Usually found in the chilled sections of Chinese supermarkets.

Dofu – see Fresh bean curd

Dofu ru – see Fermented bean curd

Dried chilli flakes (spice)

These are made from dried whole red chillies, including the seeds, which are crushed into flakes – they give a fiery heat when added to dishes.

Dried Chinese mushrooms (dried)

These have a strong aroma and need to be pre-soaked in hot water for 20 minutes before cooking. They have a slightly salty taste and complement savoury dishes well. After soaking, the stem can be left on or discarded. Available from Chinese supermarkets. Use dried shiitake or porcini mushrooms as a substitute.

Dried seaweed/Nori (dried)

This is sold in thin sheets. It is usually roasted over a flame until it turns black or purple to green before it is packaged. Nori can be used as a garnish or to wrap sushi. Once opened, the pack must be sealed and stored in an airtight container, or the nori can lose its crispness. If this happens, just roast the sheets over an open flame for a few seconds until crisp.

Chinkiang black rice vinegar (condiment)

Made from fermented rice, this strong aromatic vinegar comes from Jiangsu province, where it is produced in the capital, Nanjing. The taste is mellow and earthy and, when cooked, it gives dishes a wonderful smoky flavour. Balsamic vinegar makes a good substitute. Available from Chinese supermarkets.

Cinnamon stick/bark (spice)

This is the dried bark of various trees in the *cinnamomun* family, one of the more common being the Cassia tree.

It can be used in pieces or ground. Ground cinnamon adds a sweet woody fragrance to any dish. Cinnamon is also said to have health-giving properties, such as preventing the common cold and aiding digestion.

Cloves (spice)

The clove tree is an evergreen and its dried flower buds are the aromatic spice that is one of the components of Chinese five-spice powder. Cloves are strong and quite pungent. They are also used in Traditional Chinese Medicine to help digestion and promote the healthy function of the stomach, spleen and kidneys.

Congee (dish)

A type of plain soupy rice or rice porridge. Can be combined with

Dried shrimp (dried)
These are shrimp that have been pre-cooked and then dried and salted to preserve them. To use, soak in hot water for 20 minutes to soften them, then drain. Orange-red in colour and very pungent in aroma and taste, they come in packets. As with all preserved ingredients, it is best to store them in an airtight container. Available from Chinese supermarkets.

Edamame beans (fresh/frozen)
Edamame are green soy beans that are harvested while the beans are still attached to the bushy branches on which they grow. 'Eda' means 'branches' and 'mame' means 'beans' in Japanese. The pods are cooked whole and the seeds are then squeezed out. Available fresh or frozen.

Egg noodles (fresh/dried)
The most common type of noodle, they are made from egg yolk, wheat flour and salt and come in various thicknesses and shapes. Some are flat and thin, others are long and rounded like spaghetti; some are flat and coiled in a ball. Available in various dried and fresh varieties. Store the fresh variety in the fridge for up to 5 days.

Enoki mushrooms (fresh)
These are tiny, white, very thin, long-stemmed mushrooms with a mild delicate flavour. When raw, they give great texture to salads. When lightly steamed, they are slightly chewy. They require very little cooking.

Fennel seeds (spice)
Fennel is a strong aromatic spice that has a slight aniseed aroma and flavour, but is much sweeter. It is one of the ingredients in

Chinese five-spice powder. Delicious when toasted or pan-fried and added to dishes.

Fermented bean curd (dofu ru) (preserved)
This is bean curd that has been preserved and flavoured with chilli, salt and spices. It is often cubed, comes in many flavours and white and red varieties are available. It is quite strong in flavour and is eaten on its own or used as a marinade, condiment or an accompaniment to congee. It can be found in glass jars in Chinese supermarkets.

Fermented salted black beans (dried)
These are small black soya beans that have been preserved in salt and so they must be rinsed in cold water before use. A common ingredient, they are used to make black bean sauce and can be found in Chinese supermarkets. Only substitute with black bean sauce if you can buy a very good-quality one, otherwise the dish won't taste the same.

Fish ball/Fish cake (fresh)
The fleshy meat of white fish is combined with spices, salt and flour and made into fish balls or cakes, which are then fried or steamed and vacuum-packed ready to cook. Great added to stir-fries and soups. You can usually find many varieties in the Chinese supermarket with different flavourings, and you can also buy squid or cuttlefish balls, as well as vegetarian varieties.

Five-spice powder – see Chinese five-spice powder

Fresh bean curd (dofu/tofu) (fresh)
Described as the 'cheese' of

China, fresh bean curd is made from protein-rich soya bean curd. It is white and quite bland, but takes on the flavour of whatever ingredients it is cooked with. It is used as a meat substitute in a vegetarian diet. In Japan it is called tofu and in Chinese, dofu. The texture is quite creamy and silky and there are various varieties, such as firm, soft and silken. The firm variety is great in soups, salads and stir-fries. Silken has a cream cheese-like texture. Dofu is protein-rich and contains B vitamins, isoflavones and calcium. The fresh variety is usually found in the chilled sections of Chinese supermarkets and can be kept chilled in the fridge for up to one week.

Gailan – see Chinese kale

Garlic chives (jiucai) (fresh)
Also known as Chinese chives, these have long, flat green leaves and a strong garlic flavour. There are two varieties, one with small yellow flowers at the top and one without. The flowers can be eaten. Both are delicious used in soups and stir-fries. Available from Chinese supermarkets.

Groundnut oil (oil)
This pale oil is extracted from peanuts and has a subtle, nutty flavour. It can be heated to high temperatures without burning and is great to use in a salad dressing. As an alternative, use vegetable oil.

Hoisin sauce (sauce)
This is made from fermented soya beans, sugar, vinegar, star anise, sesame oil and red rice (which gives it a slight red colour). This is great used as a marinade and as a dipping sauce.

Jasmine rice (dried)

This is a long-grain white rice that originates from Thailand. The rice has a nutty jasmine-scented aroma and makes a delicious accompaniment to dishes. As with most rice, you need to rinse it before cooking until the water runs clear to get rid of any excess starch. White and silky, this rice when cooked is soft, white and fluffy.

Light soy sauce (condiment)

Light soy sauce is used in China instead of salt. It is made from fermented soya beans and wheat. A versatile and staple ingredient, it can be used in soups, stir-fries and braised and stewed dishes. Wheat-free varieties, called tamari, are available for those with wheat intolerance, and there are also low-sodium varieties for those watching their sodium intake.

Longjing tea (tea)

'Longjing' means 'Dragon well' and is the name of the area where this famous tea is grown in the Hangzhou region. A mild green (unfermented) tea, it has a gentle sweet flavour and a pure aroma. It is high in antioxidants and contains vitamin C and amino acids. Available at good tea

shops, online, or from Chinese supermarkets.

Lychee (fruit)

Red or amber in colour, oval in shape and with a brittle skin, lychees are the fruit of an ever-green tree native to southern China. The translucent white or pinkish flesh is aromatic and has a distinctive flavour. In the centre is a largish seed. Available fresh or tinned.

Mijiu rice wine (condiment)

'Mi' means 'rice' and 'jiu' means 'wine'. A strong rice wine made from fermented glutinous rice, it is clear in colour and has a high alcoholic content, between 19% and 25%. Some varieties are sweet and served as a dessert liqueur. Great used in cooking, too. Can only be found in Chinese supermarkets. As an alternative, use vodka or gin.

Miso paste (soya bean paste)

This is a thick paste made from fermenting rice, barley, soya beans, salt and a fungus called kojikin. It comes in many varieties depending on the types of grains used to ferment the paste. It is used in Japanese soups and stocks and is sweet, earthy, fruity and salty.

Mung bean noodles (dried)

Made from the starch of green mung beans and water, these noodles come in various thicknesses. Vermicelli is the thinnest type. Soak in hot water for 5–6 minutes before cooking. If using in soups or deep-frying, no pre-soaking is necessary. They become translucent when cooked. Great in salads, stir-fries and soups, or even in spring rolls. Vermicelli rice noodles can be used as a substitute.

Oyster mushrooms (fresh)

This fungi is oyster-shaped, moist, hairless and fragrant, and comes in different colours – white, yellow and grey. It is soft and chewy with a slight oyster taste – great in a stir-fry.

Oyster sauce (sauce)

This seasoning sauce made from oyster extract originated in the Canton province in China. It is used liberally on vegetable dishes and can be used as a marinade. A vegetarian variety is also available. This is a very salty ingredient so taste the dish before adding.

Pak choy (fresh)

This is a vegetable from southern China. The broad green leaves, which taper to white stalks, are crisp and crunchy. It can be boiled, steamed or stir-fried.

Pickled chilli bamboo shoots (pickle)

Bamboo shoots that have been pickled in vinegar, salt and chilli oil. They're great when used to flavour soups and stir-fries. They can usually be found in glass jars in Chinese supermarkets.

Panko breadcrumbs (ingredient)

Produced in Japan, and made from bread without crusts, these have a crisper texture than other breadcrumbs. They are available from Asian stores and many large supermarkets.

Potato flour (ingredient)

Potatoes are steamed, dried and then ground to give this silky smooth white flour. It gives wonderful crispness to ingredients when they are coated in it before being shallow- or deep-fried. It is gluten free. Sometimes called potato starch, it is available from

Chinese supermarkets and some supermarkets.

Preserved mustard greens/ Pickled Chinese cabbage (pickle)
The roots and leaves of the mustard cabbage are preserved with plenty of chilli and salt. They are available in jars, tins or packets from Chinese supermarkets.

Rice vinegar (condiment)
Plain rice vinegar is a clear vinegar made from fermented rice. It is used in dressings and for pickling and is more common than black rice vinegar. Cider vinegar can be used as a substitute.

Roasted soya beans (dried)
These are soya beans that have been cooked and dry-roasted to give them a crunchy texture. They're great as a garnish. They can be bought ready to eat from the health grain section of super-markets or in health food shops. Alternatively, use dry-roasted peanuts.

Rock sugar (dried)
These large sugar crystals are slightly golden-yellow in colour. They are used like granulated sugar in Chinese cooking. Use half the quantity of soft brown sugar as a substitute.

Satay sauce (sauce)
Not to be confused with Thai peanut satay sauce, this spicy salty sauce is made from dried shrimps, chillies and spices. This makes a great ingredient in a stir-fry, or mix with soy sauce, chillies and fresh herbs for a delicious dipping sauce. Available from Chinese supermarkets.

Sesame oil – see Toasted sesame oil

Sesame paste (paste)
This is made from crushed roasted white sesame seeds blended with toasted sesame oil to give a golden brown paste, and is used with other sauces to help flavour dishes. If you cannot find this rich sesame paste, you can use tahini (the Middle Eastern equivalent) instead, but it is a lot lighter in flavour and so you will need to add more toasted sesame oil. Available from Chinese supermarkets.

Sesame seeds (ingredient)
These oil-rich seeds come from an annual plant, *Sesamum indicum*. They add a nutty taste and a delicate texture to many Asian dishes. Available in black, white/yellow and red varieties, toasted and untoasted.

Shaohsing rice wine (condiment)
This is wine made from rice, millet and yeast, which has been aged for between three and five years. Rice wine takes the 'odour' or 'rawness' out of meats and fish and gives a bittersweet finish. Dry sherry makes a good substitute.

Shi wheat flour noodles (dried)
'Shi' means 'thin/fine'. They are available in white and yellow varieties. The yellow variety has added colouring. They're great in soups, salads and stir-fries. Use egg noodles as a substitute. Available from Chinese supermarkets.

Shiitake mushrooms (fresh)
These large dark-brown mushrooms are umbrella-shaped fungi that are prized for their culinary and medicinal properties. They contain all eight essential amino acids in more significant proportions than soya beans, milk, meat and eggs, as well as vitamins A, B, B12, C and D, niacin and minerals. They are a staple in China, Japan and other parts of Asia and are a popular source of protein.

Sichuan chillies/dried chilli flakes
There are many different varieties of Sichuan chillies – a common type is a short, fat, bright red chilli that is hot and fragrant. They are usually sun-dried. You can grind the whole chillies in a pestle and mortar to give flakes.

Sichuan peppercorns (spice)
Known as 'Hua jiao' in Mandarin or 'flower pepper', these are the outer pod of a tiny fruit. They are widely used all over China and especially in western China. Can be wok-roasted, cooked in oil to flavour the oil, or mixed with salt as a condiment. They have a pungent citrusy aroma.

Sichuan preserved vegetables – see Preserved mustard greens

Smoked paprika (spice)
Mild to red-hot peppers are smoke-dried over wood and then ground to a powder. The powder has a distinct flavour and aroma. Sweet, hot and mild varieties are available.

Snake beans (fresh)
Snake beans or long beans are mostly grown in Asia. They are long, plump green beans, sometimes with a purple tinge to them, and since they are quite long, some varieties tend to twist. The fatter beans are more tender and sweet when cooked. This nutritious bean contains beta-carotene, vitamin C and phosphorus, and the Chinese use this plant to make tonics for ailing kidneys or for stomach problems. They make a great accompaniment to many dishes.

Spring roll wrappers/pastry (fresh)
Made from wheat flour and starch, these are used for wrapping foods such as spring rolls before deep-frying. Available in the frozen sections of Chinese supermarkets. If you can find the type made with coconut oil and salt, they can be eaten raw, filled with salad and with dressings. deep-fried or pan-fried. Filo pastry makes a good substitute.

Star anise (spice)
A staple ingredient in Chinese cooking, these are called 'Bajio' or 'eight horns' in Chinese. They are the fruit of a small evergreen plant that grows in southwest China. The star anise has an aniseed flavour and is one of the ingredients found in Chinese five-spice powder.

Toasted sesame oil (condiment)
Made from white pressed and toasted sesame seeds, this oil is used as a flavouring and is not suitable for use as a cooking oil since it burns easily. The flavour is intense, so use sparingly.

Tofu – see Fresh bean curd

Turmeric (spice)
This is a tuberous rhizome of the ginger family. The rhizomes are first cooked for several hours and then dried before being ground into a powder, deep yellow in colour. Turmeric imparts a strong yellow colour to any dish and gives a slightly mustardy, peppery, earthy flavour. It also has medicinal properties and is used for its antiseptic properties for cuts and burns.

Vermicelli mung bean noodles – see Mung bean noodles

Vermicelli rice noodle (dried)
Similar to vermicelli mung bean noodles, they come in many different widths and varieties. Soak in hot water for 5 minutes before cooking to soften. If using in salads, soak for 20 minutes. If using in a soup, add them dry. They turn opaque white when cooked. Great in soups, salads and stir-fries.

Wasabi (fresh/powder)
A Japanese variety of green horseradish, more fiery than the white. Combine wasabi powder with warm water to make a paste, or add warm cream.

Water chestnuts (tinned)
Water chestnuts are the roots of an aquatic plant that grows in freshwater ponds, marshes and lakes, and in slow-moving rivers and streams. Unpeeled, they resemble a chestnut in shape and colouring. They have a firm, crunchy texture. Sometimes available vacuum-packed, they are mostly sold in tins.

Wheat flour dumpling wrappers/skins (fresh/frozen)
Made from wheat flour, water and salt, these are flat thin discs of finely rolled dough used to make dumplings. They can be found in the frozen or chilled sections of any Chinese supermarket. When using, keep covered with a damp towel to prevent them from drying out.

Wheat flour flat udon noodles (dried noodles)
This is a thin, white wheat flour noodle. Do not confuse these with the thick Japanese udon noodle. They are great in soups, salads and stir-fries.

Wheat flour pancakes (fresh)
Made from wheat flour, water and salt and rolled into very thin discs, these are steamed before serving and accompany Peking duck and other dishes. They can be found in the frozen or chilled sections of any Chinese supermarket.

Wheat starch (dried)
Obtained from wheat grain. This white silken powder is combined with hot water and used to make dumpling skins that turn from opaque white to translucent white once steamed.

Wonton wrapper (fresh/frozen)
Made from egg, wheat flour, salt and water, they are used to make dumplings. They can be bought fresh or frozen from any Chinese supermarket.

Wood ear mushrooms – see Chinese wood ear mushrooms

Yellow bean sauce (sauce)
This is made from fermented yellow soya beans, dark brown sugar and rice wine. It makes a great marinade for meats and as a flavouring in many savoury dishes.

Index

A

adzuki red beans/red bean paste 211

  tang yuan with sweet red bean soup 202, **203**

apricot and plum dipping sauce 181

aromatic beef noodle soup 194, **195**

aubergine, spicy Sichuan 119

B

bacon

  chicken, smoky bacon and bamboo shoot stir-fry 58, **59**

  razor clams with lardons and bamboo shoots **98**, 99

  spicy bacon crispy haddock **88**, 89

bamboo shoots 211

  chicken, smoky bacon and bamboo shoot stir-fry 58, **59**

  prawn and chilli bamboo shoot stir-fry 111

  razor clams with lardons and bamboo shoots **98**, 99

beef

  aromatic beef noodle soup 194, **195**

  Chongqing beef 72

  garlic chilli pepper beef and mushroom pak choy 76, **77**

  rice wine pepper beef noodles **148**, 149–50

  roast beef in 'four-spiced' chilli oil **74**, 75

  saucy beef dofu 73

  Sichuan chilli bean beef stew 201

  Sichuan chilli roast beef 190–1

black beans

  black bean razor clams 103

  chicken and black bean stir-fry 47

  lobster in black bean beer sauce 196–7

  oriental mushrooms and dofu in garlic black bean sauce 120, **121**

  breaded haddock with Sichuan pepper, chilli and salt 91

butter batter prawns 18

C

Cantonese-style duck with rice 151

Cantonese-style sweet and sour pork 30, **31**

century duck eggs with coriander and mushroom sauce 19

century eggs 211

chicken

  chicken and black bean stir-fry 47

  chicken and snake bean stir-fry 44, **45**

  chicken rice 141

  chicken, smoky bacon and bamboo shoot stir-fry 58, **59**

  cold spicy chicken salad with hot dressing 56

  curry chicken stir-fry 62–3

  fried sweet chilli chicken 54, **55**

  Hainanese chicken rice **198**, 199–200

  hot pink pepper/black pepper chicken **50**, 51

  juicy chilli chicken and cashew nut 60, **61**

  steamed chicken with sour and spicy dressing and spinach 52–3

  Taiwanese ginger and sesame chicken noodle soup 144–5

  three-cup chicken 57

  yellow bean and honey roast chicken 184–5

chilli bean paste 211

  chilli bean cod 84, **85**

  Sichuan chilli bean beef stew 201

chilli oil 211

  roast beef in 'four-spiced' chilli oil **74**, 75

  Sichuan spicy pork and prawn wontons in Sichuan chilli oil 177–9, **178**

chilli sauce 211

Chinese beer 211

  lobster in black bean beer sauce 196–7

Chinese cabbage 211

  pork with Chinese leaf 26, **27**

Chinese five-spice powder 211

Chinese wood ear mushrooms 211

Chinkiang black rice vinegar 212

Chongqing beef 72

cinnamon stick/bark 212

citrusy salad 131

cloves 212

cod

  chilli bean cod 84, **85**

  ginger, chilli and soy-steamed cod 90

  sweet and smoky 'hong sao yu' 92, **93**

cold spicy chicken salad with hot dressing 56

congee 212

coriander, fresh/seeds 212

crabmeat

  crabmeat sweetcorn soup with black truffle 10

  Shanghai-style crabmeat and egg noodle 136

  shrimp, crabmeat, dofu and spinach soup 11

crispy Mongolian lamb 68–9
crispy twice-cooked pork *36*, 37–9
cumin 212
curry chicken stir-fry 62–3
curry powder 212

D

daikon (white radish) 212
dark soy sauce 212
deep-fried dofu 212
dofu *see* fresh bean curd
dofu ru *see* fermented bean curd
dried chilli flakes 212
dried Chinese mushrooms 212
dried seaweed/Nori 212
dried shrimp 213
duck
    Cantonese-style duck with
        rice 151
    duck spring rolls 180–1
    Peking duck *186*, 187–9
    sweet and sour duck 48, *49*
dumplings, pork and water
        chestnut 182–3
duo-duo lo 161

E

edamame beans 213
    spicy red cabbage and edamame
        beans 128, *129*
egg-fried rice 155, *155*
egg noodles 213
eggs
    egg and tomato spring onion
        stir-fry 123
    Grandfather's egg, mixed
        mushroom and celery broth 12
    saucy pork and tomato egg
        stir-fry 32
    Shanghai-style crabmeat and
        egg noodle 136
    sweetcorn egg and spring onion
        stir-fry
enoki mushrooms 213
exploding river prawns 100–2,
    101

F

fennel seeds 213
fermented bean curd (dofu ru)
    213

dofu ru haddock 83
fermented salted black beans 213
fish balls/fish cake 213
    mixed seafood crispy noodle
        138, 139–40
fresh bean curd (dofu/tofu) 213
    oriental mushrooms and dofu in
        garlic black bean sauce 120,
        121
    saucy beef dofu 73
    sea bass and dofu clear soup 7
    shrimp, crabmeat, dofu and
        spinach soup 11
fried pork cutlet 29
fried sweet chilli chicken 54, *55*

G

garlic chilli pepper beef and
    mushroom pak choy 76, *77*
garlic chives 213
garlic pak choy exotic mushroom
    stir-fry 127
garlic spinach 122
golden needles: Grandma's pork
    and golden needle soup 8, *9*
Grandfather's egg, mixed
    mushroom and celery broth 12
Grandma's pork and golden
    needle soup 8, *9*
griddled honey yellow bean pork
    34, 35
groundnut oil 213

H

haddock
    breaded haddock with Sichuan
        pepper, chilli and salt 91
    dofu ru haddock 83
    spicy bacon crispy haddock
        88, 89
Hainanese chicken rice *198*,
    199–200
Hoisin sauce 213
hot pink pepper/black pepper
    chicken *50*, 51

J

jasmine rice 214
    boiled 154, *154*
    Cantonese-style duck with
        rice 151

chicken rice 141
    egg-fried 155, *155*
    Hainanese chicken rice *198*,
        199–200
    Mum's sweet potato jasmine
        rice 137
    spicy fragrant minced pork with
        pickled soy 'lettuce', spinach
        rice 152, *153*
juicy chilli chicken and cashew
    nut 60, *61*

L

lamb
    crispy Mongolian lamb 68–9
    spicy chunky lamb *70*, 71
leeks, crispy 15–17
lei-cha 171
light soy sauce 214
lobster
    in black bean beer sauce 196–7
    in hot garlic spinach sauce
        192, 193
longjing tea 214
lotus root crisps 125
lychee 214
    lychee and strawberry spring
        rolls with vanilla ice cream and
        golden syrup 163–4, *164*

M

mango
    mango and sago sweet soup 160
    mango coconut coulis 167
    passionate passion fruit and
        mango cheesecake 170
menus 206–9
mijiu rice wine 214
miso paste 214
mixed seafood crispy noodle
    138, 139–40
monkfish: sweet and sour fillets
    86–7
Mum's sweet potato jasmine rice
    137
mung bean noodles 214
mushrooms
    garlic chilli pepper beef and
        mushroom pak choy 76, *77*
    garlic pak choy exotic
        mushroom stir-fry 127

Grandfather's egg, mixed mushroom and celery broth 12
oriental mushrooms and dofu in garlic black bean sauce 120, *121*

N

noodles
aromatic beef noodle soup 194, *195*
mixed seafood crispy noodle *138*, 139–40
rice wine pepper beef noodles *148*, 149–50
Shanghai-style crabmeat and egg noodle 136
Taiwanese ginger and sesame chicken noodle soup 144–5

O

octopus: wok-fried with garlic coriander salsa 104, *105*
orange and green tea loaf cake *204*, 205
oriental mushrooms and dofu in garlic black bean sauce 120, *121*
oyster mushrooms 214
oyster sauce 214

P

pak choy 214
crispy 'seaweed' 15–17
garlic chilli pepper beef and mushroom pak choy 76, *77*
garlic pak choy exotic mushroom stir-fry 127
panko breadcrumbs 214
passionate passion fruit and mango cheesecake 170
Peking duck *186*, 187–9
'Piantung' 29
pickled chilli bamboo shoots 214
pickled Chinese cabbage 215
pineapple
pineapple sorbet with mango coconut coulis 167
skewered pineapples 168, *169*
pork
Cantonese-style sweet and sour pork 30, *31*
crispy twice-cooked pork *36*, 37–9

fried pork cutlet 29
Grandma's pork and golden needle soup 8, *9*
griddled honey yellow bean pork *34*, 35
pork and water chestnut dumplings 182–3
pork with Chinese leaf 26, *27*
red-cooked pork 33
saucy pork and tomato egg stir-fry 32
Sichuan spicy pork and prawn wontons in Sichuan chilli oil 177–9, *178*
Sichuan stir-fried pork with cucumbers 28
spicy fragrant minced pork with pickled soy 'lettuce', spinach rice 152, *153*
sweet and sour Wuxi ribs 20, *21*
potato flour 214–15
prawns
butter batter prawns 18
exploding river prawns 100–2, *101*
mixed seafood crispy noodle *138*, 139–40
prawn and chilli bamboo shoot stir-fry 111
rice wine tomato king prawns 106
Sichuan spicy pork and prawn wontons in Sichuan chilli oil 177–9, *178*
Sichuan-style sweet and sour prawns *108*, 109–10
spicy Sichuan pepper prawn-fried rice 142, *143*
squid and crevettes in chilli tomato sauce 107
preserved mustard greens 215

R

razor clams
black bean razor clams 103
with lardons and bamboo shoots *98*, 99
red cabbage
spicy red cabbage 126
spicy red cabbage and edamame beans 128, *129*
red-cooked pork 33

rice *see* jasmine rice; wild rice
rice vinegar 215
rice wine pepper beef noodles *148*, 149–50
rice wine tomato king prawns 106
roast beef in 'four-spiced' chilli oil *74*, 75
roasted soya beans 215
rock sugar 215

S

salad
citrusy 131
cold spicy chicken with hot dressing 56
spicy wild rice 146, *147*
salsa, garlic coriander 104
satay sauce 215
saucy beef dofu 73
saucy pork and tomato egg stir-fry 32
scallops
wok-fried crispy 15–17, *16*
yellow bean scallops and chives 13
sea bass
sea bass and dofu clear soup 7
steamed wine sea bass 82
sesame flatbread 69
sesame oil *see* toasted sesame oil
sesame paste 215
sesame seeds 215
Shanghai-style crabmeat and egg noodle 136
Shaohsing rice wine 215
shi wheat flour noodles 215
shiitake mushrooms 215
shrimp, crabmeat, dofu and spinach soup 11
Sichuan chilli bean beef stew 201
Sichuan chilli roast beef 190–1
Sichuan chillies/dried chilli flakes 215
Sichuan peppercorns 215
Sichuan spicy pork and prawn wontons in Sichuan chilli oil 177–9, *178*
Sichuan stir-fried pork with cucumbers 28
Sichuan-style sweet and sour prawns *108*, 109–10
skewered pineapples 168, *169*

smoked paprika 215
snake beans 215
  chicken and snake bean stir-fry 44, *45*
soup
  aromatic beef noodle 194, *195*
  crabmeat sweetcorn with black truffle 10
  Grandfather's egg, mixed mushroom and celery broth 12
  Grandma's pork and golden needle 8, *9*
  mango and sago sweet 160
  sea bass and dofu clear 7
  shrimp, crabmeat, dofu and spinach 11
  Taiwanese ginger and sesame chicken noodle 144–5
  tang yuan with sweet red bean 202, *203*
  traditional-style hot and sour *4*, 5–6
soy sauce *see* dark soy sauce; light soy sauce
soya beans *see* edamame beans; roasted soya beans
spicy bacon crispy haddock *88*, 89
spicy chunky lamb *70*, 71
spicy fragrant minced pork with pickled soy 'lettuce', spinach rice 152, *153*
spicy red cabbage 126
spicy red cabbage and edamame beans 128, *129*
spicy Sichuan aubergine 119
spicy Sichuan pepper prawn-fried rice 142, *143*
spicy wild rice salad 146, *147*
spinach
  garlic spinach 122
  lobster in hot garlic spinach sauce *192*, 193
  shrimp, crabmeat, dofu and spinach soup 11
  spicy fragrant minced pork with pickled soy 'lettuce', spinach rice 152, *153*

steamed chicken with sour and spicy dressing and spinach 52–3
spring roll wrappers/pastry 216
spring rolls
  duck 180–1
  lychee and strawberry with vanilla and golden syrup 163–4, *164*
squid
  squid and crevettes in chilli tomato sauce 107
  Taiwan-inspired 'teriyaki' squid *112*, 113
star anise 216
steamed chicken with sour and spicy dressing and spinach 52–3
steamed wine sea bass 82
store cupboard 210
sweet and smoky 'hong sao yu' *92*, *93*
sweet and sour duck 48, *49*
sweet and sour monkfish fillets 86–7
sweet and sour Wuxi ribs 20, *21*
sweet potato: Mum's sweet potato jasmine rice 137
sweetcorn
  crabmeat sweetcorn soup with black truffle 10
  sweetcorn egg and spring onion stir-fry 118

T
Taiwan-inspired 'teriyaki' squid *112*, 113
Taiwanese ginger and sesame chicken noodle soup 144–5
tang yuan with sweet red bean soup 202, *203*
three-cup chicken 57
toasted brown rice jasmine green tea 165
toasted sesame oil 216
tofu *see* fresh bean curd
tomato
  egg and tomato spring onion stir-fry 123

rice wine tomato king prawns 106
saucy pork and tomato egg stir-fry 32
squid and crevettes in chilli tomato sauce 107
traditional-style hot and sour soup *4*, 5–6
turmeric 216

V
vermicelli rice noodles 216

W
wasabi 216
water chestnuts 216
  pork and water chestnut dumplings 182–3
wheat flour dumpling wrappers/skins 216
wheat flour flat udon noodles 216
wheat flour pancakes 216
wheat starch 216
wild rice
  spicy Sichuan pepper prawn-fried rice 142, *143*
  spicy wild rice salad 146, *147*
wok-fried crispy scallops 15–17, *16*
wok-fried octopus with garlic coriander salsa 104, *105*
wonton wrappers 216
wontons, Sichuan spicy pork and prawn in Sichuan chilli oil 177–9, *178*
wood ear mushrooms *see* Chinese wood ear mushrooms

Y
yellow bean sauce 216
  griddled honey yellow bean pork *34*, 35
  yellow bean and honey roast chicken 184–5
  yellow bean scallops and chives 13

Acknowledgements

During this past year I have received so much support for my last book and television show, *Chinese Food Made Easy*, and it has given me tremendous joy and confidence. I am extremely grateful and thankful to all cooks out there who have supported me. I would not be here without your belief. It warms my heart to know that there is a huge appreciation for delicious Chinese food and I am so pleased to be able to share it with you.

There were so many recipes I wasn't able to include in *Chinese Food Made Easy* and so I am delighted to have the opportunity to write *Ching's Chinese Food in Minutes* and include many of them here. For this, I thank the powers at HarperCollins for giving me the opportunity – Victoria Barnsley, Belinda Budge and Sally Annett, as well as the rest of the team.

I cannot thank enough the whole talented team (again). You make the process of creating a book a delight and I feel we have bonded over the many Thai (pad thai and fish-maw) lunches. Here's to you all – Susanna Abbott (my down-to-earth editorial director), Kate Whitaker (gorgeous photographer), Wei Tang (fabulous stylist), Annie Nichols (spirited stylist), my unbelievably cool and organised editor, Barbara Dixon, and the charmingly funny designer, Jacqui Caulton.

To everyone who has shaped my career – especially Jeremy Hicks and Toby Eady – thank you for championing me, for all your advice, help and support over the years and for bringing me to where I am today. I am deeply grateful. Thanks to Alexandra Henderson for believing in me and helping to open doors for me, and to Sarah Canet who has continued to provide so much support over the years. To all who continue to give me opportunities, thank you from my heart, because it allows me to do what I love.

To my prized family and my Buddhist masters – I am so lucky to have you all in my life, I don't know where I would be without you. Grandpa, Mum, Dad, En-shen, Sao Sao, Aunty, Jamie, James, June and to all the extended family in Taiwan, Hong Kong, South Africa and Malaysia. I love you all dearly and may we share more food and happy days to come.

Finally, to Pak choy and Choi sum – thanks for all your naughty bunny habits, they keep me sane when I feel insane...

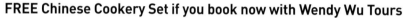